10 WAYS ANYONE CAN GRADUATE FROM COLLEGE DEBT-FREE

A Guide to Post-College Freedom

Thomas,

Thank you for your support NUPE!

8/8/23

KEVIN Y. BROWN

10 WAYS ANYONE CAN GRADUATE FROM COLLEGE DEBT-FREE

-

A Guide to Post-College Freedom

by KEVIN Y. BROWN
© 2012 Legacy Thinking Labs. All rights reserved.

ISBN: 978-0-9847671-0-6 (EPub)
ISBN: 978-0-9847671-1-3 (Paperback)

Cover Design by:
Mario Shamir
Mariosloredo@gmail.com
www.luvzombie.com

Twitter: @KevBrown1| Facebook.com/KevBrown001

Seminars by Kevin Y. Brown

AM/PM: As I Matriculate Pay Me!

Label Material Brand

Post College Freedom! (12 session program)

Start to Finish

StyleBook

Your Brand Within (10 session program)

Meet Kevin online and receive free college financial training at

www.mydebtfreecollege.com

DEDICATION

This book is dedicated to Mr. Philmore Graham and Mrs. Carrie S. Wilson—two people who changed the course of my life by exposing me to the value of education and holding me to higher standards.

AND

My dearest Marie Elizabeth Dutton Brown—without you, this project would not have been possible.

THANK YOU FOR EVERYTHING!!!

CONTENTS

www.mydebtfreecollege.com

10 Ways Anyone Can Graduate From College DEBT-FREE

"If I have to take out a loan for college, I'm dropping out!" is what I said to my dormitory hall director, Dr. Raphael X. Moffett, a few days into college. This comment was my response during a conversation that we were having about students' struggles to obtain loans and the possibility that they would be sent home because they could not meet their financial obligation.

When I said that I would drop out if I had to take out a loan for college, my hall director and the other students looked at me as if I was crazy and sarcastically wished me good luck. Dr. Moffett told me that most of the students had student loans. I quickly repeated, "I don't care; If I have to take out a loan for college, I'm dropping out." I kept that promise to myself and today I am student loan debt-free.

I have written this book because I now have an unusual freedom that most of my peers who attended college do not. That freedom is a result of zero college debt. Although my peers may earn good salaries, a considerable amount of their money goes toward repaying college loans, and they frequently tell me how much they wish they had searched for scholarships and grants while in school.

While they are stressed out about their student loan debt, I have had the opportunity to move to New York—one of the most expensive cities in the world—without having to take a job I did not want in order to repay a loan. What is even better is that my debt-free college experience has allowed me to travel abroad to England, Iceland, Jamaica, Mexico, Spain, Rome and Egypt.

I'm not saying this to brag; I am telling you this so that you can visualize what working hard to find free money for your college education can offer you versus being trapped in a job, city, or country for the next thirty years because of your student loan debt. I don't worry about the burden of monthly payments to a lender, or avoiding annoying phone calls from agencies trying to collect money from me. Truthfully, I don't want you to either, because repaying student loans can become overwhelming.

The pressure of student loan debt makes it almost impossible not to scramble to find a job as soon as you graduate. And it also increases your possibility of accepting an undesirable job that simply pays your bills. While in college, the majority of students you encounter will accept loans as the method of financing their college educations. Don't follow their lead.

By following the strategies outlined in this book, you will obtain the tools needed to fund a free college education and discover the freedom of graduating debt-free.

Why 10 Ways Anyone Can Graduate From College DEBT-FREE Is For YOU!

10 Ways Anyone Can Graduate From College DEBT-FREE is written from experience. In the chapters that follow, you will find my story and the strategies that make my statement, "If I have to take out a loan, I'm dropping out!" true.

To assure you that a free college-level education is possible, I have listed the following challenges that I faced before entering college, and the subsequent results that I achieved with the ten strategies offered in this book:

CHALLENGES

- I was raised in California's foster care system for seventeen years
- I grew up in one of the worst neighborhoods in Northern California: The Country Club Crest in Vallejo
- I achieved a 740 SAT score
- I had minimal financial support from family and friends
- I was the first in my biological and immediate foster care families to leave the state to attend a university
- I had no knowledge of the college financing system
- Because of my attitude and behavioral history, my mentors and foster parents expected me to be kicked out of college within my first week.

RESULTS AFTER IMPLEMENTING THE STRATEGIES OUTLINED IN THIS BOOK

- I double-majored in Fashion Design/Merchandising and Business Supply Chain Management
- I spent a semester abroad in London, England
- I graduated with 178 credit hours
- I was financially able to travel back and forth to California (and other states) for school vacations
- I played for Clark Atlanta University's men's basketball team
- **I obtained a FREE five-year college education valued at over $140,000!**

Considering the challenges I was faced with, if I graduated college debt-free, then you can too!

THE VALUE OF HIGHER EDUCATION:
Education vs. Income

Higher education is invaluable. Many skill-building, networking, and training opportunities are available on college campuses. Professional skill-building workshops offered on-campus are offered by major corporations, and students in leadership groups, clubs, or on athletic teams are recruited. Some of these programs are as basic as proper dining etiquette and networking with other professionals. Students often benefit from attending banquets, dinners, and events where decision-makers and sponsors are present. You can find these programs off-campus, but those who attend on-campus events will often have a higher education profile, which can make networking more beneficial.

Higher education places you within a network of people who could be tomorrow's leaders; those individuals who are striving to attain similar goals to yours offer you access to more resources than most. It also teaches you critical thinking skills and how to be culturally competent to compete in today's diverse world. I had teammates and other college friends from foreign countries such as Ghana, France, and Jamaica to name a few. Our friendships allowed me greater insight into lifestyles in places around the globe, which prepared me for my study abroad experience in London. There, I learned even more about other cultures and ways of life.

A higher education provides you with the skill set to compete with others all over the world and makes moving into management, changing jobs, or entering higher-level jobs much easier. For example, I often hear of stories about where a person has been working at a job for twenty years and applies for a management position only to lose the job to someone with a higher education who has no experience. This is not always the case but often, a degree is comparable to experience and says that a person with a higher education can handle a job because they have been taught to think critically. Hiring a person with higher education can boost the credibility of a company.

Higher education is not limited to four-year colleges. Concentrated programs, two-year degrees and other forms of training all constitute as higher education. While having a diverse background and diverse life experiences can boost the credibility of your resume, higher education is one of the most universal ways to move up financially in society.

The higher your education level, the more likely you are to be employed when the economy is in an economic downturn. Your education level affects the amount of money you can earn in your lifetime. As a high school graduate, I would earn a little over one million dollars in my lifetime. The *Median Synthetic Work-Life Earnings table* below shows the lifetime earnings of Americans according to their education level. This table is available for download at **www.mydebtfreecollege.com/resources.**

MEDIAN SYNTHETIC WORK-LIFE EARNINGS			
EDUCATION LEVEL	**MALE**	**FEMALE**	**ALL PERSONS**
NONE–8TH GRADE	$892,605.20	$596,207.60	$744,406.40
9TH–12TH GRADE	$992,935.00	$640,184.80	$816,559.90
HIGH SCHOOL GRADUATE	$1,238,902.00	$857,532.40	$1,048,217.20
SOME COLLEGE	$1,524,004.40	$1,073,985.60	$1,298,995.00
ASSOCIATE'S DEGREE	$1,668,997.20	$1,249,644.60	$1,459,320.90
BACHELOR'S DEGREE	$2,127,639.00	$1,583,705.60	$1,855,672.30
MASTER'S DEGREE	$2,691,821.00	$2,040,328.60	$2,366,074.80
PROFESSIONAL DEGREE	$3,645,609.20	$2,456,865.60	$3,051,237.40

Table 1 Median Synthetic Work-Life Earnings
Note: Synthetic work-life earnings represent expected earnings over a 40-year time period for the population aged 25–64 based on annual earnings from a single (cross-sectional) point in time. The estimate was calculated by adding median earnings for eight 5-year age groups, multiplied by five.

Source: Julian, Tiffany A. and Robert A. Kominski. 2011. "Education and Synthetic Work-Life Earnings Estimates." *American Community Survey Reports*, ACS-14. U.S. Census Bureau, Washington, DC.

*The Numbers are based on averages and do not reflect the financial reality for every person in the United States of America. People may make more or less.

STUDENT LOAN DEBT AT A GLANCE

Student loan debt is borrowed money plus accumulated interest that is owed to student loan lenders. According to Mark Kantrowitz, publisher of **www.finaid.org**, the total of student loan debt increases by about $2,853.88 per second (finaid.org), and is now over one trillion dollars in the United States. Nationally, student loan debt is now higher than credit card debt.

Many students and parents take student loans as their primary method of financing a college education because they cannot pay out of pocket or are unaware of other financing options such as grants, scholarships, or fellowships that may be available.

Some students and parents take on student loans because they find it easier to apply for a loan than complete the work that is required to apply for a scholarship. A loan can also be seen as a source of guaranteed money that most college students are using, while scholarships are seen as an opportunity to win the money to finance expenses. Sometimes, students may not have the grades to compete for merit-based aid, but it is still important to be aware of what your options are and understand that there are various methods to finance your college education without loans.

There are over ten million dollars' worth of resources listed in the high school and college scholarship sections within this book, and here is a little motivation to use them: student loan interest results in a borrower repaying lenders more than his or her initial loan.

Figure 1 illustrates the amount of money students owe by the time they graduate according to the type of college they attend.

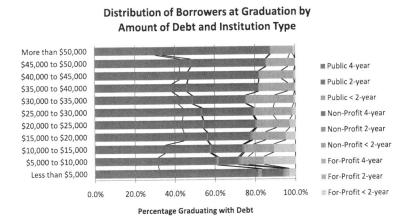

Fig. 1 Copyright ©2011 by FinAid Page LLC (FinAid.org). All rights reserved. Reprinted with permission.

Source: Kantrowitz, Mark *Distribution of Debt at Graduation by Amount of Debt, College Type and Degree Program*, September 29, 2010. (*Addendum*, October 1, 2010.)

Figure 2 shows the percentage of student loan debt that the average student has according to his or her major.

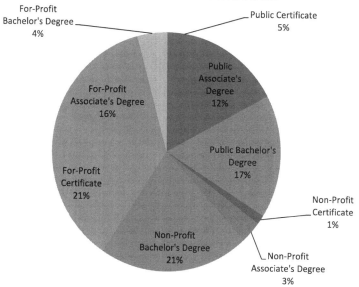

Share of Graduates with Excessive Debt

Fig. 2 Copyright ©2011 by FinAid Page LLC (FinAid.org). All rights reserved. Reprinted with permission.

Source: Kantrowitz, Mark *Distribution of Debt at Graduation by Amount of Debt, College Type and Degree Program*, September 29, 2010. (*Addendum*, October 1, 2010.)

Although two-thirds of college students have accumulated federal and private loans, you don't have to follow the majority. In this book, you have the power and the tools to be the exception to the student loan rule.

CONSEQUENCES of DEFAULTING on STUDENT LOANS

Obtaining student loan debt can have severe consequences if you are not responsible with money or don't repay your debts on time. According to www.finaid.org, student loan default happens when a borrower has failed to make payments on his or her federal student loans for 270-360 days and does not make special arrangements with their lender to get a deferment or forbearance (postponement of payment on a loan).

The reasons why a loan can go into default can vary, but the most common causes are unemployment and a person's financial mismanagement. In these instances, borrowers can set up monthly payment plans with loan lenders based upon their monthly income.

Failing to pay your student loans on time, also known as defaulting, can lead to severe and frustrating consequences. Below are nine penalties that you can be subjected to if you default on your loans:[1]

1. Administrative Wage Garnishment
If you do not voluntarily make arrangements to repay your student loan(s), up to 15% of your pay check can be taken by federal or private loan lenders without your consent.

2. Collection Costs
When you sign your promissory note before receiving your loan(s), you agree to repay your student loan lender. If you default on your loan(s), the outstanding amount will be sent to a collection agency and you will have to pay the cost for the agency collecting on your debt, which can be added to the total balance of your loan. The rates for collection costs are re-

---

[1] *"Consequences of Student Loan Default." TG Online. Texas Guaranteed Student Loan Corporation, 15 Sept. 2011. Web. 22 Oct. 2011.*

calculated annually and the percentage rate is subject to change due to administrative costs, or the assignment of your account to other collection agencies. Keep in mind that the adjustment in your rate can increase or decrease your total balance due.

3. License Suspension

There are many states that allow professional and vocational boards to refuse to certify, certify with restrictions, suspend, or revoke a member's professional or vocational license. In some cases, states allow professional and vocational boards to impose fines on members if they default on their student loans. License suspensions are applicable to the legal, healthcare, teaching, insurance, state, and commercial fishing professions.[2]

4. Credit Reporting

TransUnion, Experian, and Equifax are the three credit bureaus that can be notified of the original amount and current balance of each of the student loans that you default on. A loan(s) in default will continue to show up on your credit report for seven consecutive years after the original date of delinquency.

5. Reinstatement of Eligibility for Federal Student Aid

Once a student loan is declared in default, you no longer have the option for deferments or forbearances. In addition, you cannot receive any additional Title IV* federal student aid until you have made approved payments for a minimum of six consecutive months.

6. Withholding of Transcripts and Academic Records

Each school has its individual policy for releasing academic records. Some schools may require additional documentation or verification of your current repayment status before releasing academic records such as enrollment/attendance records, academic transcripts, certificates, degrees, etc.

---

[2] *"License Revocations | Student Loan Borrower Assistance." Student Loan Borrower Assistance | A Resource for Borrowers, Their Families and Advocates. National Consumer Law Center. Web. 22 Oct. 2011.*

7. Treasury Offset Program

When you are eligible to receive a federal tax refund from the federal government, this money can be garnished to repay your defaulted student loan(s).

8. You Can Be Sued

The government and private lenders can sue you to collect up to the entire amount of your student loan(s). There are no time limits on when the government and private lenders can sue you to collect student loan debt.

9. Your Federal Benefits Can Be Taken

The government can garnish your federal benefit payments (Social Security and Social Security Disability benefits (SSDI)) as reimbursement for any student loan that you default on. These benefit garnishments exclude Supplemental Security Income (SSI) and can be executed without a statute of limitations. (Lockhart v. U.S. (04-881) 546 U.S. 142 (2005)

Consider and use these penalties as your motivation to research and apply for scholarships and grants in order to avoid the headaches of repaying student loans.

Title IV funds include all federal financial aid program funds. Examples are: Pell Grant, Federal Supplemental Educational Opportunity Grants (FSEOG), Academic Competitiveness Grants (ACG), National Science and Mathematics Access to Retain Talent (National SMART), Teacher Education Assistance for College and Higher Education Grants (TEACH), Leveraging Educational Assistance Partnership (LEAP) and Special LEAP (SLEAP) Grants, Direct Loan Program, Federal Perkins Loans, Work-Study)

TYPES OF FINANCIAL AID

Financial Aid is funding given to students by the government for educational expenses including tuition, books, room and board. There are two types of financial aid: 1) merit-based and 2) Need-based.

Merit-Based Aid: Financial aid that anyone can receive no matter his or her level of need.

Merit-based financial aid is free money that comes in the form of scholarships. These can be awarded to students by any college, university, or outside organization for special talents, outstanding academic achievements, or leadership potential. In some cases, scholarships are renewable.

Need-Based Aid: Financial aid based on your needs.

Need-based aid requires that a form, The Free Application for Federal Student Aid (FAFSA), be filled out by both undergraduate and graduate students in the United States to determine their eligibility for loans, federal and state grants, and work-study programs.

Loans are funds borrowed to pay for college expenses that **must be repaid** with interest to lenders. There are five types of federal loans:

- Federal Perkins Loan
- Federal Stafford Loan
- PLUS Loan for Parents
- PLUS Loan for Graduate and Professional Degree Students
- Consolidation Loan

Grants are funds disbursed by the state and federal government that **do not have to be repaid**. There are four types of grants:

- Federal Pell Grant
- Federal Supplemental Educational Opportunity Grant (FSEOG)

- Teacher Education Assistance for College and Higher Education (TEACH) Grant
- Iraq and Afghanistan Service Grants

Work-Study is a federal student job program that allows students to earn money while enrolled in college to help fund their educational expenses.

Scholarships are funds that do not have to be repaid. Scholarships can be athletic or academic-based and are disbursed through your college/university, a fraternity, sorority, alumni association, or through many other sources inside and outside of your campus community.

This next section entails the strategies which I personally used to graduate college debt-free. When you read beyond this point you are making up your mind that you are going to give your DEBT-FREE college journey all you have. GO FOR IT!

10 WAYS ANYONE CAN GRADUATE FROM COLLEGE DEBT-FREE

1

EXCEL IN HIGH SCHOOL

Attending school for seven or more hours a day and squeezing in time to hang out with friends can sometimes blur your connection between high school and college. Yes, college is definitely an enjoyable place to be, but your academic performance, conduct, and extra-curricular activities in high school can dictate to which colleges you get accepted, and can also affect the type of college experience you have. When your high school transcript reflects high grades, an upward trend in higher grades, and/or honor classes, you will receive more college acceptances and more college scholarships.

While in high school, I was disciplined, made an effort to earn good grades, and developed good study habits. As a result of my hard work, Clark Atlanta University (CAU) paid me to attend.

Good academic performance may often help you avoid the consequences of any bad conduct. However, once you reach a certain age and are in certain academic environments, your conduct is expected to reflect your capability. This is a time when it no longer pays to be the bad boy or girl. You will be competing with others who do not hide their intelligence with foolish behavior. In fact, you may find that while many of your peers are not as smart as you, they know how to conduct themselves in a way that gives the impression that they are top performing students. Sometimes this is accomplished by being quiet or saying less than everyone else. In short, it pays to act as smart as you are.

If you are anything like I was and are not too familiar with how to conduct yourself in certain environments, it may be in your best interest to become involved in positive extra-curricular activities. Often, these are the places where you can observe many kids and parents who know how to conduct themselves, and they can assist you.

Although excelling in high school is one of the smartest ways to earn a free college education, it may not always be the easiest. There are many distractions such as girls, boys, and peer pressure, but keep in mind that your main job is to focus on your grades. It's required by law that you attend high school, so you might as well do your best. You may not see it now, but your conduct and academic performance in high school will impact your life well after you graduate.

Becoming an A/B student may not be easy for everyone, and that's okay. Keep in mind that just because a course is challenging, it doesn't make it impossible to attain good grades. Whether you are taking Honor or Advanced Placement (AP) courses, or studying for countless hours, tutoring and homework resources are available.

Seeking help from a tutor is not a bad thing. Think of tutors as coaches or mentors. What professional dancer, athlete, or musician do you know who doesn't have a coach to help them improve their skills? A tutor is a teacher, and if you do not have a coach/tutor to help you improve yourself and your skills, then you are not really trying to be the best that you can be. Are you maximizing your potential by asking for help? Those subjects that you may be struggling with now could be beneficial in the future.

You can maximize your potential by maintaining a high grade point average (GPA). Hanging out with friends whose goals are to be successful and productive can expand your experiences as well as open doors for you that otherwise might be closed. For example, participation in leadership classes, honor societies, social clubs, athletics, and community service activities can help others and build your network and character. Although some extra-curricular activities do not require a minimum GPA, you can always use your academic GPA to gain access to anything you want; your GPA and conduct are your passports to new places and opportunities. Positive and productive extra-curricular activities are where most of your peers who are focused on being their best and having great futures will be. It is exciting to surprise people with your high GPA. The look of approval on their faces is always priceless.

The scholarship application process can be time-consuming but the preparation for this and your college education begins in high school. Developing your reputation, academic and extra-curricular activity performance are important elements in maximizing scholarship opportunities and your college experience. It could mean the difference between repaying student loans and a debt-free post-college life!

Author's Experiences and Opinions:

- _Various opportunities and a positive circle of peers can provide you with access to information, people, and experiences that can propel you to the next level. Below is an example of how hanging out with a positive friend took me to a higher level._

  In high school, I lived in one of the worst neighborhoods in Vallejo, California, but no one could tell by looking at my *transcript. My teachers, principal, and athletic coaches were all aware of my academic capabilities, but they were also aware of my poor behavior. I needed to make some changes, so I joined the leadership class, began to volunteer in school and the surrounding communities, and created new and positive relationships with other kids who were doing positive things and achieving their goals.*

Ironically, most of the other kids who were doing well and preparing for their future happened to be from the other part of town far from my neighborhood. As our friendships grew stronger, I began to see more of what life was like from their perspective, as well as their parents'. They invited me to their nice homes, where there were bigger TVs, better food than I ate at home, lots of books, and a peaceful environment. Their conversations were frequently centered on future life plans and goals; they knew leaders in the city who had access to scholarships, and also knew which colleges were best to attend.

Generally, there were more constructive things to do at their houses. Activities that I considered a privilege, such as going into the refrigerator whenever I wanted, cooking whatever I liked, using the family car, or conversing about a difference of opinion with parents, were activities that my friends considered normal. My experience with different friends, their families, and the observations of their households inspired me to want more out of life. It also granted me more access to gatekeepers: people who could improve my circumstances by giving me important information for scholarships and other tools that I needed to excel.

When administrators and teachers saw me running errands or helping with activities for other staff members, they made a mental note of it. If they didn't, I reminded them. And that helped me to access scholarship information, free transcripts, administrative assistance, and other privileges.

- *By maneuvering intelligently through high school e.g. making friends with those in charge and their secretaries, and spending your time with people who are constantly striving for brighter futures, your high school community will be supportive. They will consider you one of their own. They'll want to push you to excel so that you can be one of their success stories. Why? Because it makes what they do more meaningful.*

- *The great thing about applying for scholarships while in high school is that you can accumulate several scholarships to pay for college expenses prior to enrollment. For example, I applied for and received a $2,000 General Mills scholarship during my junior year of high school. Then, after participating in the Boys and Girls Club and volunteering in the community and maintaining a 3.0 GPA, I re-applied during senior year and won the same amount. This gave me a total of $4,000 to use toward college tuition and textbooks before I began my freshman year of college.*

- *Preparation for your free college education begins in high school; the habits that you develop will carry over into college. Excel in high school so that you are prepared to excel in college.*

2

SACRIFICE

Whenever focusing time and energy into achieving a goal, such as obtaining a scholarship or 4.0 GPA, you may find yourself sacrificing another activity or desire. Each sacrifice has its challenges and some may make you question the purpose of your goal. When this occurs, embrace it and think about the bigger picture in order to understand why you are making the sacrifice.

Achieving a debt-free college education will come with many challenges, but you can overcome them to achieve the following:

- The freedom to travel and live anywhere you want after college without limiting your options due to accumulated student loan debt.
- The ability to begin saving or achieving your desires with your earnings after college instead of repaying lenders.

Four sacrifices that you may have to endure on your debt-free college journey:

- **Time at Home** – Realize that life-changing events such as births, deaths, health issues of family and friends, etc. occur during your college years.
- **Social Time** – Partying and hanging out with friends.
- **Luxury Lifestyle** – Extra spending money, nice clothes, dining out, etc.
- **Immediate Gratification** – You will do the hard work (applying for scholarships, getting good grades, and making the right connections) up front to reap the benefits of not having to repay college loans.

While in college, you may spend more time away from home than you ever have. During this time, whether days, hours, or months, things at home will change. New people will move into your neighborhood, childhood friends may move away, or a family member's health may improve or worsen, and others may even die. You may be there to witness these events, or you may be away working towards a better future for yourself and your family.

It is very important at times like these to separate your goals from what is happening at home. So often, this is a very difficult decision, but the time that you spend on assignments, improving your work ethic, or networking, can mean the difference between being financially stable after college or not.

While in college, the grass may seem greener for those who chose not to attend because they will often have access to money, cars, clothes, and a lifestyle that may be attractive to you at the moment. This may cause you to ask yourself, *why am I studying and broke when I can have things that others have now?* You must answer this question by telling yourself that you are working to place yourself in a position to be able to have a lifestyle better than what you are currently witnessing.

Pursuing a debt-free college education might be one of the poorest times in your life, but I can assure you that if you stay the course and complete your DEBT-FREE college education, there are strong possibilities that you will have all of the things that you desire and so much more—including priceless experiences that will bring you friends who share your same ambitions in life. College is one of the best sacrifices I have ever made and I loved it so much that I would do it all over again.

Another necessary sacrifice in order to achieve a debt-free college education is balancing your time. If your peers are financing their education with student loans then they appear financially stable for the time being, but remember that they must begin repaying the money they borrowed (with interest) six months after graduation. Over the years, the amount initially borrowed can double or triple. To reach your debt-free college goal, you must work harder than other students, maintain a high average, constantly research scholarships, and network with influential people while your peers may be hanging out, taking trips, or relaxing.

Each student's schedule and priorities will vary according to personal preferences. You may have to sacrifice hanging out and sleeping-in to work toward your post-college freedom. You will have to decide whether to chill, hangout and take the loans offered to you. I suggest making the sacrifice to work hard up front. While it took a lot of dedication and balance, I definitely had fun while working hard on my DEBT-FREE college journey, and you can too; it just takes balance. (See Strategy 4: Master Your Schedule.)

Yes, you will miss out on some parties, relaxation, and sleep, but those who work hard are barely seen because they are always working, and this can make their presence more valuable. Have you ever heard the phrase *absence makes the heart grow fonder*, which suggests that people miss you more when you are not around? This fact is one reason why the paparazzi get paid so much for photographs of celebrities who happen to be some of the hardest working and successful people. The paparazzi get paid because it is hard to see celebrities everywhere. Missing some events and being inaccessible at times can cause others to be more interested in what you are up to. Being unavailable to hang out and missing social events due to working to become your best is the norm for the top achievers in every profession.

If you sacrifice a little bit of relaxation and play time, you will be able to save your money in order to build your wealth after college.

Sacrifice also means understanding delayed gratification, which is sacrificing something up front to receive the benefits of your sacrifice later. You will be faced with decisions that will require sacrifice continuously throughout your college days. Often, your sacrifice will be related to the topics mentioned at the beginning of this chapter: time at home, social time, luxury lifestyle and immediate gratification. When faced with these decisions you must try to do what will serve you best overall and enable you to reach your goals. There will always be another party or time to relax but you have four to five key years to make decisions that can save you headaches and assure your financial freedom after college.

Many say a DEBT-FREE college education is impossible, but I stand with a select group of people who can tell you from experience that it is very possible. The decision is yours to make.

One of the best ways to keep sight of your DEBT-FREE college education goal is to completely understand why you are willing to work toward the goal. To do so, complete a "Why Sacrifice" worksheet, which will allow you to visualize and anticipate the challenges, sacrifices, and pros and cons of obtaining your debt-free college education. The following is an example of what a completed "Why Sacrifice" worksheet looks like.

WHY SACRIFICE WORKSHEET

My goal: To graduate college debt-free

My anticipated sacrifices:
1. Partying and hanging out as much as everyone else
2. New clothes
3. Time at home
4. Dining out
5. Trips and vacations

Why I am willing to make these sacrifices:
1. Because I want to be free to do what I want after I graduate
2. Because I want to keep the money I earn
3. Because I do not want to take out student loans and have to repay lenders
4. Because when I graduate I want to be able to immediately help my family financially without hindering myself

Pros of achieving my goal:
1. I will be a college graduate
2. I can make more money than I typically would without a degree
3. This is a milestone
4. I will not owe any student loan vendors any money
5. I will have post-college freedom
6. I am free to travel and do as I wish because I don't have any debt and I don't have to take the first job offered to me
7. I will be stress free

Cons of not achieving my goal:
1. I will graduate college, but I'll have to begin to repay loan lenders six months after I graduate
2. I may have to take any job I can get just to start paying back my debt
3. I may experience high levels of stress trying to figure out how to pay back student loans
4. I may be in debt for the rest of my life due to the interest rates on my loans and how long it takes me to repay them.

Your "Why Sacrifice" worksheet is very important and I suggest keeping it in a safe place so that you can look at it whenever you feel that you cannot achieve your goal because of its challenges. I used this technique to keep my eye on my DEBT-FREE college prize and the cool thing is that it helped me to accomplish other goals in addition to my debt-free college education.

To help yourself reach your debt-free college goal, download the "Why Sacrifice" worksheet from the book's website **www.mydebtfreecollege.com/resources.**

Author's Experiences and Opinions:

- *Sacrificing time at home is something that comes with the territory of achievement. Many things changed when I was in college over 2,000 miles away from home. Jeremiah, my oldest nephew, was growing up and I only saw him during Christmas breaks or summer vacations. I missed some of his early years because graduating college debt-free was my number one priority.*

  Also, while I was away in college, two of my friends died and I wasn't able to attend their funerals. Some family members became sick while others recovered from serious illnesses; one of my mentors lost his memory, and a few of my friends were starting families and businesses.

  During these times of sorrow and happiness, I had to stay focused in order to stay committed to my goal of graduating college debt-free. It was a huge sacrifice to miss so much while being away. Who knows where I would be if I weren't away in college focused on my future? The sacrifice of being away from home also taught me that my family and friends would survive while I was away. When things became really challenging for me I used my "Why Sacrifice" list to stay focused.

- *There is always the opportunity to study abroad while in college and leaving the country can be a hard decision. I thought long and hard before I left for London for a quarter. My decision to study abroad placed me over 5,400 miles from my family and hometown, but the experience was more than worth it.*

- *During my junior year of college, I had to make a really tough decision. I was a fashion design major and every year during my college's homecoming week, the fashion department assisted in the production of a fashion show. This show was a big deal and very instrumental in a fashion student's understanding of fashion show production. Fashion majors also received credit for participating.*

During one of our practices, my basketball coach told the team that if any of us missed practice because of the homecoming fashion show, we would be kicked off of the team. He was still upset from the previous season because one of the players missed practice to model in the fashion show. After practice, I went to speak with my coach to plead my case. I told him that I would have to miss practice for the fashion show because it was a part of my curriculum as a fashion design major. He responded by telling me that he meant what he said: If anyone misses practice because of the homecoming fashion show they are going to be kicked off of the team. Period. I went back to discuss the matter with my coach a few more times and even spoke with the assistant coaches to try to get him to change his mind, but he wouldn't budge.

Finally, the day of the fashion show came, and I had to make a decision. Something was going to be sacrificed. I remember thinking to myself; do I sacrifice my grades or my athletic scholarship that I worked two years to earn? I reflected on what I was taught growing up in the Continentals of Omega Boys and Girls Club, and chose my academics over athletics. I worked the show, received my course credit, showcased my clothing line and got kicked off the team all in the same day.

This was a hard decision to make. I had always wanted to play college basketball and being on the team as a potential captain was a dream come true. But it all had to be sacrificed for my academics and debt-free college goal. It was an undesirable sacrifice to make but one that I am happy I made.

As a result of no longer being a part of the team, I focused heavily on my clothing line and academics for the rest of my junior year, and returned to the team the following year after a poor season and negotiations with the coach.

- *During my fourth year of college, there was a time when my money was low. I did not have enough money to eat. Instead of making my friends, mentors, or family members aware, I kept quiet about my situation because I wanted to figure it out for myself. One day when I was walking on campus down "the strip" (a long walkway where students hang out that divides the entire Clark Atlanta University Campus), someone whom I had seen around campus but who did not attend CAU approached me with a proposition. He told me that because I knew so many students, he could pay me $2,000 a week if I sold drugs for him. I quickly thought to myself, I could really use this kind of money.*

As great as the deal sounded, I knew that it could not be that simple, and that I was not going to throw away my future and all of the hard work that people invested in me. I refused to place myself in a position where I might have to return home to Vallejo, California, a statistic or disappointment. So I told him that I wasn't interested and went on about my day. I really could have used that money but it wasn't worth jeopardizing how hard I had worked to get to where I was.

Soon after his proposition, something great happened. A friend reimbursed the money I had lent to him—money that I had forgotten about. So everything worked out for the best. That proposition to deal drugs was truly a test of my character. I sacrificed the fast way of solving my financial problem to be the upstanding student that my mentors, community, and family could be proud of. The rewards are far better than they would have been had I agreed to sell drugs. No one can call me an ex-drug dealer and I take pride in that. My decision to not sell drugs is one that I will never regret.

- If your funds ever become so low that you can't afford meals, let your friends, family, and mentors know. Desperate times call for desperate measures, and you don't want to be in a position where you are so desperate that you are willing to jeopardize your future in order to survive. Many students fall on hard times, but true friends and family will often assist you without judgment if you do not abuse their generosity.

- I was in college for five years because I decided to double major and study abroad during the semester that I was due to graduate. As a result, my second major required an additional year. I had already done my semester budgeting (Strategy #10 Be Financially Smart) and course forecasting (Strategy #7 Master Your Schedule) before I decided to pursue additional academic opportunities.

3

BUILD RELATIONSHIPS

Building relationships with people is often overlooked, but it can be beneficial when it comes to financing your education. It is also natural and necessary for maintaining emotional stability.

A financial aid officer will make an extra effort to provide aid that is available to people they know. It is your responsibility to develop relationships with key people who know how to access money for tuition and expenses and who have connections that can assist in paying for your higher education.

This is one of the most important strategies in this book. Most of my scholarship money was obtained by building relationships with key people such as department chairs, financial aid officers, professors, and others.

Think about building relationships the same way you'd think about receiving money from your family. Who are your family members most likely to give their money to? You or a stranger? Almost anyone would give money to family members or people they know before offering it to a stranger.

This is the same mentality you must have with your financial aid counselor. They may not be your parent or family member, but you can be sure that they will give the scholarship money that becomes available to their family, close friends, or people they know before they give it to strangers.

It may not sound fair, but this is the way things work. If you just meet with your financial aid counselor when you need something, why should you be treated any differently from other students? People take care of those they know, and your institution's financial aid advisors, people with influence, and scholarship committees are all operated by caring people.

I'm not suggesting that you try to use your financial aid counselor. Rather, you should build a genuine relationship so that your counselor has a personal connection with you. Your relationship with him or her can actually be the difference between having and not having student loan debt.

My "mom" in the financial aid office took great care of me as if I were really her child. I treated her as if she were really my mom. Her treatment led other staff members to treat me with kindness and respect, and as a result, I continued to receive scholarship money. I kept my grades high and participated in many extracurricular activities, which were the ways I showed my appreciation and support for the assistance they provided.

Knowing that I had someone whom I could talk to because of the relationships that I had built on campus made me feel safer and helped me to continue to excel because I knew I had a support group. Being able to discuss and learn about certain aspects of life with friends totally changed my life.

When people help you, show them your appreciation by doing better than you were before. In the case of your debt-free college education, show your appreciation through proper decorum and academic achievement.

There were students with higher GPAs than mine who could have taken my scholarship away from me. But, based on the fact that I was a well-rounded student with a strong relationship with my financial aid counselor, I was repeatedly awarded institutional and outside scholarships.

Building relationships goes beyond your financial aid counselor. Research and observe who else has influence in the areas in which you need assistance. For example, if there is a scholarship available through your academic department, who would be an understanding and supportive advisor? It may be the department chair or a senior professor. If you don't know who has influence, find out and pay attention to the things that are important to them also. It is not always all about you. **Remember:** It's your job to have the proper relationships with these decision-makers so that they know who you are when the time comes to award students with scholarships. When appropriate, you should also periodically remind these gatekeepers of your financial need, because there are thousands of students in need of money for school, but many of them are not willing to create and nurture genuine relationships.

When you create stable and nurturing relationships you feel safer to be yourself. You feel that you have people who actually care about your well-being. Feelings of comfort and a sense of family when you are away from home can help you to perform better academically and build better relationships.

There is one platinum rule that you will need to follow when building relationships and that rule is: *Be Genuine!* People can sense insincerity. If they sense that you aren't genuine, then you are worse off than you were when they didn't know you.

<u>Author's Experiences and Opinions:</u>

I received an institutional scholarship consecutively for the following reasons:

- ***MOST IMPORTANTLY:*** *I did my best academically and met scholarship committees and financial aid counselors halfway so they could reason in my favor.*
- *I established a personal relationship with my financial aid counselor.*
- *I made a name and reputation for myself as someone who worked extremely hard to help himself, which made others want to help me.*

How to Create and Nurture Relationships with Decision-Makers:

- *Drop in just to say "hello."*
- *Express gratitude and send thank-you cards often.*
- *Offer your assistance whenever you can.*
- *Make sure that you build relationships with gatekeepers such as secretaries, department aids and work-study students. These individuals often control the access you have to people and privileges that others may have difficulty accessing. People help those who help themselves and are kind to them.*
- *Building relationships is a great way to generate funds for college, but it is also vital to your success in life. The friends you make in college may be for life and may also have connections to jobs after you graduate. Continue to build sincere relationships and a positive rapport with them.*
- *Make thank-you cards your standard.*

4

MEET EVERYONE HALFWAY

Your DEBT-FREE college education will be a result of the effort that you put into obtaining it. So, in order to gain the best opportunities for scholarship funding and access to decision-makers, you must do your part by performing your best overall and meeting everyone (e.g. scholarship committee members, counselors, parents/guardians, peers, etc.) halfway.

Meeting individuals halfway means developing the following essential elements of character and education in order to become a well-rounded person.

Meet Everyone Halfway Element #1: Reputation

People will ask others about you when they see you on campus or come across your name on applications and other materials. Most of the time, you will not be aware of their inquiries. For this reason, it is important to have and maintain a positive reputation. Assist administrators or gatekeepers with tasks in order to show them how determined you are to remain positive and take the necessary steps to obtain scholarship funding, recommendation letters, etc., that ultimately lead to a debt-free college education.

A great reputation inspires trust. People select those who they trust because they know the person will represent their cause or organization well. Your letters of recommendation will speak to your character and work ethic but you have to represent yourself beyond paper and sometimes in interviews. The better you represent yourself overall will result in more opportunities coming your way. People will also seek you out and will be more inclined to help if they hear great things about you. Everyone loves being a part of a success story. Meet everyone halfway with your reputation so that it can bring you opportunities that you were not aware of previously.

Meet Everyone Halfway Element #2: Extra-Curricular Activities

Extra-curricular activities expand your network, introduce you to new people, and expand the reach of your positive reputation. These activities sharpen your skills, mind, and ability to adapt to different environments and circumstances. People always want to know what you do outside of your personal tasks, and your extra-curricular activities demonstrate that you are dedicated to causes bigger than yourself. This is a topic often inquired about by decision-makers when you are being considered for scholarships, academic or athletic awards, or career and educational opportunities.

Extra-curricular activities also offer you life-changing experiences such as advanced learning, teachable moments, and exposure to new things. Participating in extra-curricular activities and maintaining a positive reputation will show others that you are responsible and have the ability to multi-task.

Meet Everyone Halfway Element #3: Academics

Without the grades you won't get paid. If someone likes your reputation and participation in extra-curricular activities, they can only take you so far on your debt-free college journey without your meeting them halfway academically.

In high school I had friends who broke state records in athletics but were not able to attend college on the full ride scholarships (all expense paid college educations) that were waiting for them. They could not obtain their debt-free college educations because they did not have the minimal grades or test scores for admission. They could not meet the college's/university's requirements halfway and as a result, missed out on life-changing opportunities.

During college I also witnessed peers lose scholarships because of their poor academic performances and as a result, they had to take time off from school or transfer to another college. Maintaining competitive grades is a must; you do not want to have all of the tools (athletic ability, extra-curricular activities, and a good reputation) and allow your academics or one missing element of meeting everyone halfway to be the reason why you would not be selected for or move forward with the opportunities presented to you. Advisors, selection committees, and others can pull your transcript without your knowledge and you can lose opportunities without ever being informed because you are not achieving the academic standard.

This strategy also applies to most of the things you will accomplish in life. Your hard work and determination will equip you with important skills so that you are prepared when your network(s) present you with opportunities.

Henry Hartman says, "Success always comes when hard work meets opportunity." To be successful at obtaining a debt-free college education and other opportunities in life, you must do your part and meet everyone halfway.

Authors Experiences & Opinions:

- *Meeting others halfway has resulted in many benefits. I will share a few of the experiences that this strategy has allowed me to have.*

  When I was a troubled boy on the verge of being kicked out of the Continentals of Omega Boys and Girls Club (COBGC), the founder, Mr. Philmore Graham who became my mentor, took the time to challenge me by using academics and rewards as a technique to change my behavior. He was aware of my academic reputation and rewarded me with sports cards, treats, and other items for correctly answering math and critical thinking questions. So naturally, I began to seek him out on a daily basis in order to earn rewards. The catch was that he would only reward me if I were well behaved. This technique made me meet Mr. Graham halfway by improving my behavior and learning more. With my response to his curriculum-based challenges, I was able to stay in the COBGC program, which resulted in building my academic and social foundation.

  In high school, when my ninth grade photography teacher, Ms. Wilson stopped me to ask if I was going to college I told her, "No, I don't have any money or family; I may go to a community college or something." She knew about my academic reputation and responded with, "Oh yes you are; you have too much potential to throw away."

Ms. Wilson made it her business to make attending college a reality for me. She spent many hours teaching me how to fill out college applications, scholarships, and the FAFSA. Each time that she showed me something new, I would research it and return with questions or have the task completed, thus encouraging her to teach me more.

I was willing to help myself and Ms. Wilson was willing to continue helping me. I also had the academics and extra-curricular activities, and was working on my reputation, so Ms. Wilson was not wasting her time by helping me.

When I got to college, Ms. Batey, my professor in the Fashion department, helped me to find money for school and went beyond her teaching duties to teach me more than she was required. Because of my work ethic, Ms. Batey stayed after class to teach me and allowed me to meet her at her weekend sewing classes to learn more. She would often nominate me for opportunities because I possessed all three elements to meet her or any other person to whom she referred me halfway.

When it was time for me to move to New York City after graduating college, one of my mentors, Ms. Evelyn "Heart Lady" Polk, financed my living arrangements for my first two months because she trusted me to move to New York, work hard, make a mark, and establish a life here. She knew of my work ethic and expected nothing less. I came to New York and did what she expected—I met her halfway.

I have many, many more stories of how meeting others halfway has helped me on my journey. Trust me: I would not be here today or be able to write this book if I did not do my part and present myself as a person who could handle any task put in front of me to the best of my ability.

This is a life lesson that is bigger than just a debt-free college education. I strongly encourage you to do your part, come correct, and MEET EVERYONE HALFWAY. Keep in mind that it took time to build relationships (Strategy #3) with each of the people whom I previously mentioned I met halfway.

5

APPLY FOR SCHOLARSHIPS

Scholarships are free competitive funds. There are two different types of scholarships: renewable and non-renewable. A renewable scholarship can last more than one semester or academic year. A non-renewable scholarship only lasts for the current semester or academic year. Winning a renewable scholarship is a bonus because you have a higher chance of winning it again due to scholarship committees being familiar with whom you are and your familiarity with their specific scholarship process. Be sure to apply for both types of scholarships with the same effort.

There are thousands of scholarships to apply for and millions of available dollars. Scholarships are free to research, so you shouldn't pay anyone to find scholarships for you. Instead, you should meet with your high school guidance counselor to discuss what scholarship deadlines, if any, are approaching or are ongoing. You can also check with your local organizations, surf the Internet, and visit your local library for various scholarships that best fit you and your goals. To get you started, here are five popular scholarship websites:

- **http://www.scholarships.com**
- **http://www.collegeboard.org**
- **http://www.collegetreasure.com**
- **http://www.uncf.org**
- **http://www.fastweb.com**

The key to winning scholarships is to apply to more than one. It is a numbers game. Applying to one $60,000 scholarship is great, but think about how many other students are applying for the same scholarship. Do not underestimate smaller scholarship awards of $500 or $1,000, because they add up and may be less competitive than larger scholarships.

Another way to think about smaller scholarship amounts is to consider the fact that winning ten different scholarships worth $200 each is the same as winning one $2,000 scholarship.

Apply for as many scholarships as you can. You can also increase your chances of winning free money by applying for scholarships that are unique to you or your background, such as your race, family history, life experiences, hobbies, etc.

For some renewable and non-renewable scholarships, you can use the same information or documentation, but you may need to tweak your essay to fit the requirements of each scholarship. To keep a renewable scholarship, you should maintain or increase your level of academic and extra-curricular performance. Most scholarships usually have similar core requirements such as a minimum grade point average (GPA), an essay, letters of recommendation, transcripts, and records of community service and social/extra-curricular activities.

Also, continue to look for scholarships after you are enrolled in college. Ask your friends which scholarships they are applying for in order to maximize your chances. After all, you can never have enough free money.

Some scholarships organizations can run out of funding. Should you lose a $3,000 scholarship due to economic hardships on behalf of the sponsor, and you need $3,000 to enroll loan-free for the current semester, having another $3,000 scholarship available because you made the effort to apply for various scholarships from different sponsors, will help you stay debt-free, and will motivate you to continue applying for scholarships!

Often, institutional scholarships that you were not eligible for when you entered college may become available once you show that you are performing at a higher academic level, or because of your participation in extra-curricular activities. Apply for institutional scholarships every semester, every quarter or at every opportunity.

When you are awarded a scholarship, always send a thank you letter to your scholarship sponsor. If more than one person has helped you with your scholarship process, send out multiple thank you letters. Gratitude is always appreciated and remembered. Thank you letters can help move you to the top of the list for the next award term, or win you recognition with a scholarship committee.

Applying for scholarships While Meeting Everyone Halfway

Most people will not be great at all three of the meet everyone halfway elements (reputation, extra-curricular activities and academics). This is where you can become a competitor and steal the show and free money.

You want anyone who inquires about you regarding these three elements to be able to check you off as a great candidate and grant you quick access to proceed further with the opportunity. The easier it is for selection committees, academic and financial aid advisors, or anyone else to check your name off as a great candidate they can trust, the more they will throw your name into other opportunities when asked for candidates to nominate. Why? Because you have made it easy for them by meeting them halfway.

The three elements of meeting everyone halfway that are mentioned in the previous strategy will assist you tremendously in your goal of achieving a debt-free college education. To fully grasp how the Meet Everyone Halfway strategy applies to obtaining scholarships, compare it to persuading your parents/guardian to let you go to a party.

When you want to attend a party you will:

1. Find out exactly who is having the party
2. Obtain the party's location and directions so that you don't get lost
3. Figure out what it will take for your parents to say yes

Once you know all of this information, you will do what is necessary to accomplish your goal, which will most likely include:

1. Doing all of your chores
2. Behaving well in school and in public
3. Doing extra housework

By meeting your parents halfway, it will be hard for them to tell you no. Ironically, this strategy will also assist you in obtaining college scholarships. To see a side by side comparison review the getting to a party and getting a scholarship example which is also available for download on the book's website **www.mydebtfreecollege.com/resources.**

HOW TO GET TO A PARTY

1. Find out who's, when, where, what type of party it is (do you have to bring a gift)
2. Find out what it will take for your parents to tell you yes.
3. Meet Everyone Halfway: Do your chores, behave in school, at home and in public. Complete all homework/ class work and turn it in on time.
4. Wait for a decision from your parents/ guardian (putting the ball in their court and presenting yourself as the most deserving daughter/son to attend the party.)
5. Assist where you can to make sure you arrive on time. (Find the directions to the party instead of waiting for your parents/guardian to figure them out.)

HOW TO GET A SCHOLARSHIP(S)

1. Find out who's, when, where, what type of scholarship it is.
2. Find out what it will take for the scholarship committee to tell you yes you've been awarded the scholarship (requirements)
3. Meet Everyone Halfway: Complete the scholarship application, retrieve your transcripts, letters of recommendation, essay etc. Turn in the application on time
4. Wait for a decision from the scholarship committee (putting the ball in their court and presenting yourself and your application as the best candidate for the scholarship)
5. Assist where you can to make sure your application is submitted on time. Create drafts of recommendation letters, take parts of the application to be signed off on or completed by others etc.

In meeting everyone halfway, you may have to go further in order to meet your goal. You may have to assist the scholarship committee; teacher/professors who are writing your letters of recommendation who are busy while you are working on a deadline. Your deadline is most important to you because you need the recommendations. Always make tasks for others as easy as possible. This also shows initiative.

To obtain your debt-free college education, you must find the resources nearest and available to you. Next, you must do the work in order to prepare to use the resource(s). This means that you must do all that you can on your part in order to present yourself and your scholarship application professionally to the person/committee in charge.

Additional tips to meet everyone halfway for scholarships:

- Take the initiative to make the connections with people with influence; set appointments, have lunch, have conversations with them to let them know who you are.
- Get your grades to a level where they can compete with other students for free money, join groups and organizations.
- Always finish applications or respond to opportunities as quickly as possible, before deadlines.
- Always have your letters, essays or any work proofread before submitting. (Use the English writing labs on campus, which are usually free)
- Always present your materials and yourself professionally and thoroughly
- Always go back and ask questions if you have them
- Always look to grow and become better, people help those who are helping themselves
- Always show up with knowledge of anything that you are applying for or involved in. This means doing research, prior to the event or meeting.

- Your reputation and peer group all have an impact on how you are perceived on campus. You basically want administrators and peers to know that you are a good person, that you handle business in and out of the classroom and that you should be the first to be recommended for any opportunity. With a good image, you will not have to ask for help as often because people will be looking to help you. It's not always who you know but who knows or knows about you. People observe your attitude and behavior; so be your best at all times.

- If a scholarship requires a 3.0 GPA and there are thirty applicants all with a 3.0 GPA or higher, then the scholarship committee will select the recipient(s) based on other criteria specified in the application. Additional information such as your scholarship essay, community service, leadership clubs, and extra-curricular activities make you a stronger candidate for any scholarship you apply for. Your GPA gets your foot in the door and your extra-curricular activities and overall profile keep the door open. Don't be left outside because your grades can't get you in.

Author's Experiences and Opinions:

- *When seeking scholarship money to finance my debt-free college education, I did the following:*

1) *Met individuals halfway by:*

    a) *Having a great reputation*
    b) *Being involved in volunteer and extra-curricular activities*
    c) *Earning competitive grades*

2) *Identified who was in charge of free money for school (sought information from the financial aid office, department offices, professors, online research, etc.).*

3) *Found scholarships for which I was eligible.*

4)   *Researched the requirements to obtain the award.*

5)   *Knew the key person in charge of the scholarship. After securing an introduction, I established a relationship with that person and inquired about the scholarship.*

6)   *Collected the required materials (essay, letter(s) of recommendation, transcript, etc.,)*

7)   *Had my materials proofread well before the deadline.*

8)   *Requested that the key contact review the application. (The application was already read by an excellent proofreader.)*

The reason why I would ask the scholarship key contact person to review my application is so that he or she feels that they have input, which will make them care about it more. It also demonstrates the high level of effort that I am capable of doing early in the scholarship process.

9)   *Made my final application adjustments.*

10)   *Submitted the application before the deadline and all the scholarship committee had to do was say yes or no because I completed and submitted a thorough and professional application.*

11)   *Followed up with thank you cards to anyone involved in my scholarship process and checked on the award decision periodically.*

12)   *Repeated this strategy continuously.*

Download the My Debt-Free College Scholarship checklist from the book's website **www.mydebtfreecollege.com/resources.**

Here are some additional things that I would do to meet everyone halfway for scholarships:

- *I would always ask for letters of recommendation or any application materials I needed from someone early.*
- *I would always ask for general letters of recommendation so I could use them for multiple purposes.*

- *I would always ask my recommenders if they needed me to write a draft letter that they could easily modify or if they would like a list of the content/ my accomplishments that needed to be expressed in the letter. This saved my recommenders time, helped me meet my deadline and helped me get a letter that says exactly what I needed it to. This is a three in one deal.*

- *I would always make tasks as easy for the other party as possible. For example, if one of my recommenders, advisors or anyone involved in my scholarship application process would say they needed to take something over to be signed by another person whether it was for me or not, I would volunteer to go and do it. This way they did not have to waste their important time doing something so small just for me and so that I could get what was important to me done faster.*

- *I would ask any questions that I had even if I had to keep coming back every day. This showed them that I seriously wanted scholarship money and was willing to work for it.*

- *After a while, people started to send me opportunities because they knew I was qualified (the three meet everyone halfway elements) and how hard I was willing to work/working to find money for school (my reputation).*

- *My grades were much higher in college than they were in high school because I was more serious about my academic performance. I applied and won an institutional scholarship after I was in college and continued to receive the same award every year until I graduated. I didn't have this same scholarship when I first enrolled at my university but my thank-you letters and (strategy #4 meeting everyone halfway) helped me to keep it.*

6

SUBMIT YOUR FAFSA EARLY

When it's time to go to college, in order to be considered for need-based aid such as free federal and state student grants, work-study, and loans, undergraduate and graduate students must submit a Free Application for Federal Student Aid (FAFSA).

Two important factors that determine how much aid you receive are **1)** your expected family contribution (EFC)[3] and **2)** the amount of time it takes you to submit your FAFSA[4]. If you are a dependent student, you will need copies of your parent/guardian's tax return information from the previous year to complete your FAFSA application. If you are an independent student, you will need copies of your personal tax return information from the previous year to complete your FAFSA application.

If you or your parent/guardian has a delay receiving tax return information the information on your/their W2 tax forms can be used as an estimate to complete the FAFSA application and your estimate can be modified when you receive your tax return. Although the most important thing is completing your FAFSA application as soon as possible, filing your taxes is just as important because they are used to determine your EFC.

---

[3] *The Expected Family Contribution (EFC) is a measurement of your family's financial strength and is calculated according to a formula established by law. Your parent or guardian's taxed and untaxed income, assets, and benefits (such as unemployment or Social Security) are all calculated using the formula. Your family's size and the number of family members who will attend college or vocational school during the same year are also considered. You can use the calculator on www.finaid.org to get an estimate of your EFC.*

[4] *For more information about the FAFSA form or process, visit www.fafsa.gov*

To find out if you are a dependent or independent student, visit **www.fafsa.gov**. Be quick and thorough with your FAFSA application; it becomes available January 1st of each year.

Think of the FAFSA as a sweepstakes where the prize is free money to fund your education and you and two million other college students across the United States are all eligible to apply. To enter, you will need to be a full-time student above academic probation and prove your financial need. The earlier you submit your FAFSA, the more money there is available for you, and the sooner you will be awarded.

Applying early also allows you to get a head start on finding additional resources for funding your upcoming academic year. The later you apply, the quicker the pool of money disappears. Obtaining money for college is all about planning and being a few steps ahead of everyone else. Another reason to submit your FAFSA early is because work-study jobs go quickly. Some scholarship committees may require that you share the amount of money you receive in your financial aid package so that they can award you according to your financial need. This means that the earlier you submit your FAFSA, the faster you'll have your requirements for certain scholarships.

Once your FAFSA has been processed, you will receive a letter from your college or university's financial aid office. This important document is called your financial aid award letter. You do not have to accept everything that is in it. For example, you do not have to take the loans that may be offered if you do not need or want to do so. **You have the right to appeal your financial aid award letter!** Because it can vary from institution to institution, you'll need to contact your college's financial aid office to find out about the financial aid letter approval and appeals processes.

An example of why you might appeal a financial aid award letter is if you know that you are going to receive a large scholarship that is based on need but your financial aid award letter has a large amount of loans on it. You would appeal your letter to ask your school to reduce the amount of loans on your award letter so that your financial aid profile shows that you need the entire scholarship amount.

Keeping up with financial aid deadlines and requirements can be a challenge when you are dealing with so many other things on your busy schedule. Use the tracking financial aid worksheet to keep track of your financial aid deadlines. It is available for download on the book's website **www.mydebtfreecollege.com/resources**.

TRACKING FINANCIAL AID WORKSHEET

FORMS	DUE DATE	REQUIREMENTS	COMPLETION DATE
COLLEGE APPLICATION(S)			
FASFA			
CSS/ FINACIAL AID PROFILE			
TAX FORMS			
SCHOLARSHIPS			
OTHER			

Author's Experiences and Opinions:

- As an independent college student, I was proactive in my effort to obtain money for college, never waiting until the last minute to complete my FAFSA application. I always gathered my documents by mid to late January and completed the application far ahead of the deadline. Next, I would call FAFSA (1-800-4-FED-AID) to follow up to make sure that they didn't need any additional information. Finally, I would periodically follow up with my financial aid counselors until I found out what my award was going to be.

- **Remember:** There are over two million students applying for the same federal college funding as you. Be pro-active instead of reactive; don't wait to start gathering your documents for your FAFSA application. Have this information available so that your only task is to complete the application online as soon as possible.

7

Master Your Schedule

If you are not in charge of your schedule, no one else will be. From the moment your parents leave you to your first semester, you are solely responsible for what you achieve during college. You have the freedom to set your own schedule, wake up when you want, and pretty much do as you please.

With so much freedom also comes great responsibility. Your social, study, and personal time as well as a debt-free college education are all dependent on your mastering your schedule. Managing your courses, time, and academic performance will determine your graduation date and how much money you will pay to attend you college or university. Time management and pro-activeness during your matriculation are also essential to your debt-free college experience. This strategy is the key to you getting ahead and remaining on track to graduate on time.

During orientation, most colleges/universities provide every new student with a detailed guide that outlines every major by name, class level, number, and sometimes course description. These are the courses each student enrolling in their respective year is required to take in order to graduate with a degree in the major of study he or she selects. The name of this book may vary from institution to institution, but at my alma mater, Clark Atlanta University, it is called the Course Catalog.

When you receive your course catalog be sure to keep it in a safe place because it will be your guiding light throughout your degree program. If your institution does not provide you with a course catalog, your major's department should have a copy of the set curriculum needed to graduate in your chosen field according to the year you enrolled.

You can also check for a downloadable version of your course catalog on your college's website. There may be multiple catalogs available from previous years because course catalogs are usually updated every few years. It is very important that you keep a copy of the catalog that pertains to your matriculation year.

Your course catalog is very beneficial in the event that you want to change majors or have to take a leave of absence from college. It also outlines the criteria for re-admission and the statute of limitations on credits (i.e., how much time a student can take off before they have to re-enroll under the newest curriculum for his or her major). Be careful not to exceed the allotted time. Each college/university has its own policies on attendance; this is why your course catalog and being informed about your school's policies are very important. You never know what obstacles may arise or who will try to hold you back. If you are aware of the rules, you will be prepared for any challenges that come your way.

For example, at CAU, when a student takes a leave of absence, they must re-apply for admission. Should they wish to take any courses at another college/university, it would be best to check with the registrar (a university's administrative office that is responsible for student records, enrollment procedures, etc.) first to make sure that the courses are transferrable.

At Clark Atlanta University, after six years of time off from initial matriculation, a student seeking re-admission is required to meet any new curricular requirements that may be in effect. After eight years of non-enrollment, a student must re-apply for admission, and must re-take all courses again.

By re-enrolling under a new curriculum, you may need more time to complete your major, and there may be new classes that could require new pre-requisites. This will most likely result in your paying more money to be in school longer. Try to remain in school consistently because requirements to fulfill majors change frequently as a result of evolving technology and new industry methods.

You are responsible for your graduation!

This should remain at the front of your mind during your entire time in college. It is your responsibility to remain on track with your courses; you are the only person who can make sure that you graduate on time. Do not rely on your family, friends, or academic advisor. Think of your academic advisor as a consultant who can assist you, but cannot hold your hand throughout your matriculation. Academic advisors have many students. It is important to be pro-active in your effort to graduate because no one else is as invested in your college education as you are.

Mastering your schedule is important. Often, my friends complained about not graduating on time and blamed it on others when it was in fact their responsibility. I still have teammates who have not graduated because they did not master their schedules. They blame everyone else except themselves. Remember you must excel from start to finish.

Graduating on time requires that you know what classes you need to take, what pre-requisites are required, and what semester each class is offered. Check with your major's department, the office of the registrar, or course schedules provided at the end of every semester, for the new and updated class schedules for the next semester.

Pay attention to which classes are usually offered each semester. Knowing this information will help you plan for future class schedules ahead of time. If you have any questions about class availability, be sure to ask the professor(s) who usually teaches the course or the Registrar's office. Each semester equals more money that you must find to obtain a debt-free college education. Make it easy on yourself. Master your schedule!

Taking classes outside of your major:

When making your class schedule, always re-check the curriculum guidelines. Try to take required classes that pertain to your major before taking electives (classes that are outside of your major curriculum). If you are a business major with a concentration in marketing, and your dream job is marketing for a television station, take a few classes in the mass communications department. Electives are secondary to completing the curriculum for your major. Even though you have the freedom to pick your classes, you must do so responsibly.

The smartest way to add courses that are outside of your major to your schedule is by using *schedule forecasting*. Set up your class schedule for every semester according to your major requirements. Add in elective classes where you can. Schedule forecasting will help you to prioritize, which classes are most important and which pre-requisites are required so that you do not miss out on the courses you need to graduate.

I forecasted my schedule for my entire matriculation and made adjustments when course availability or times changed. Schedule forecasting provided me with a blueprint that helped me graduate on time. In the event that your schedule does not permit you to take specific courses outside of your major, you can always fulfill an internship within a field outside of your major.

Figure 3 is an example of what a Fashion Design major's completed *Schedule Forecasting* worksheet looks like. To stay on track to graduate, download this worksheet from the book's website **www.mydebtfreecollege.com/resources**.

SCHEDULE FORECASTING WORKSHEET

FIRST YEAR	CREDIT HRS		CREDIT HRS
Fall Semester: 16 hours		Spring Semester: 16 hours	
CART 101 Art Foundation I	3	CART 102 Art Foundation II	3
CBIO 101 Biological Science	3	CPHY-C 102 Physical Science	3
CENG 105 English Composition	3	CENG 106 English Composition II	3
CMAT 103 Algebra I	3	CMAT 104 Algebra II	3
CGED 100 First Year Seminar I	1	CGED 101 First Year Seminar II	1
CSOC Social Science Req.	3	CCIS 101 Info Tech & Comp. Appl.	3
Total Credit Hours	16	Total Credit Hours	16
SECOND YEAR			
Fall Semester: 15 hours		Spring Semester: 16 hours	
ART 201 Drawing I	3	CFAS 237 Fashion Illustration	3
CFAS 210 Principles of Fashion Industry	3	CFAS 230 Textiles	3
CENG 201/202 World Literature	3	CFAS 340 Apparel Construction II	3
CFAS 240 Apparel Construction I	3	HIS-C 202 U.S. Africa&World	3
CHIS 201 U.S. Africa&World	3	CFAS 250 Visual Merchandising	3
		CPED 101/2 Phys. Ed. Req.	1
Total Credit Hours	15	Total Credit Hours	16
THIRD YEAR (Study Abroad Option*)			
Fall Semester: Study Abroad (15 hours)		Spring Semester: 15 hours	
CHUM 228 Early Period	3	CFAS 320 Draping	3
CART 277 Computer Imaging Basics	3	STA-C 101 Fundamentals of Speech	3
CFAS 220 History of Costume	3	CFAS 360 Fashion Apparel CAD**	3
CFAS 310 Flat Pattern	3	Foreign Language Req. II	3
Foreign Language Requirement. I	3	CPSY 211 General Psychology	3
Total Credit Hours	15	Total Credit Hours	15
FOURTH YEAR			
Fall Semester: 15 hours		Spring Semester: 15 hours	
CFAS 440 Retail Management	3	CFAS 420 Fashion Show Production	3
CFAS 350 Fashion Accessory Design	3	CFAS 480 Internship	3
Fashion Elective	3	CFAS 410 Fashion Design Senior Col.	3
CPHI/CREL Philosophy/Religion Req.	3	CFAS 450 Fashion Design Portfolio	3
Open Elective	3	Open Elective	3
Total Credit Hours	15	Total Credit Hours	15

Figure 3 Schedule Forecasting worksheet

Time and Schedule Management:

Mastering your schedule goes beyond taking the correct courses in the correct order. It also helps with time management. Creating a master schedule that will help you get ahead during the semester will make your student life much easier and more enjoyable.

Most professors will provide you with a syllabus, an outline of the course and schedule of all work due for his or her class. If you bring all of your syllabi together to plan out which assignments are due first, and complete the small assignments while chipping away at the bigger projects early, it will save you time and headaches. Completing assignments in sections before their deadlines is a lot easier than procrastinating or cramming a day or two before they are due.

The two strategies that we will be using to fill in the master schedule are *assignment scheduling* and *study blocks*. To create an assignment schedule, you must organize the assignments on your syllabi by due dates and study time needed to complete each assignment. If you are uncertain, ask your professor how much time that they think a student should spend in order to complete and submit a completed assignment. For your peace of mind, always try to overestimate the amount of time an assignment will take to complete.

Study blocks are set amounts of time to focus your undivided attention on one subject matter (e.g. English, math, science, etc.). When using study blocks, and in order to use your time most effectively, you have to avoid distractions such as the internet (unless needed for the assignment), phone, peers, music, etc.

Studying in blocks of time with assignment scheduling will allow you to manage and execute the amount of time it will take you to complete a project. For example, if you have an assignment that is going to take five hours to complete and you have a week to finish it, you would mark the assignment's due date on your master schedule and then block out the amount of time per day that you are going to spend completing it. So a five-hour assignment that is due in a week can be broken down into the following different study blocks:

1) Five hours in one day

2) Two and a half hours for two days

3) One hour each day for five days

4) Forty-five minutes for six days

Staying on track with study blocks can also help you to visualize how much social and personal time you have. In college, classes have credit hours which are also called units and at most universities, the maximum credit hours a student can take per semester is eighteen. In some cases, more credit hours can be taken with special permission.

What follows is an example of how an assignment schedule would look for one month. (You will have to do this for every month of the semester.) For this example, we will imagine that a student has received all of his or her syllabi for their classes during the fall semester, and after organizing them, they wrote down or typed out their assignment schedule like the example on the next page.

Assignment Schedule

*MWF = Monday, Wednesday, Friday *T, TH = Tuesday, Thursday

CLASS	TIME	DAY	ASSIGNMENTS DUE	EST. STUDY TIME NEEDED	DATES DUE
Psychology 101	8-9AM	MWF	1 exam, 1 quiz	9 HRS TTL: 7, 2 HRS	10/2, 10/29
History 201	12:05PM-1:40PM	MWF	1 paper, 1 exam, 1 quiz	15 HRS TTL: 5, 8, 2	10/17, 10/24, 10/30,
English 102	10AM -12PM	T,TH	(2) 10-page papers	5 HRS/ EACH	10/8, 10/25
Art History 100	1PM-2:30PM	T,TH	1 major project	20 HRS	10/31,

After organizing their assignment schedule, the student should mark the assignment due dates on the master schedule. Their next step would be to plan their study blocks according to the estimated required study time to complete their assignments before they are due. The master schedule would look something like the example on the following page.

Master Schedule

Sunday	Monday	Tuesday	Wednesday	Thursday	Friday	Saturday	HRS SPENT STDYG
	1 Psych. 101 = 8-9am / Hist. 201 12-140pm / 30 MINS ENG. PAPER / 1 HR PSYCH. EXAM / 45 MINS ART HIST. PROJ	**2** Eng 102=10-12pm / Art Hist. 100 = 1-230pm / 1.5 HR ENG. PAPER / 1 HR PSYCH. EXAM	**3** Psych. 101 = 8-9am / Hist. 201 12-140pm / 30 MINS ENG. PAPER / 1 HR. HIST. PAPER	**4** Eng 102=10-12pm / Art Hist. 100 = 1-230pm / 1.5 HRS. ENG. PAPER / 1 HR PSYCH. EXAM	**5** Psych. 101 = 8-9am / Hist. 201 12-140pm / 2 HRS ART HIST. PROJ	**6** 2 HRS ART HIST. PROJ	12 HRS 45 MINS
7 1 HR ENG. PAPER / 1 HR PSYCH. EXAM	**8** Psych. 101 = 8-9am / Hist. 201 12-140pm / 1 HR PSYCH. EXAM / 2 HRS HIST PAPER / 45 MINS ART HIST. PROJ / 10 PG ENG. PAPER DUE/ 5 HRS STUDY TIME	**9** Eng 102=10-12pm / Art Hist. 100 = 1-230pm / 1 HR ENG. EXAM / 3 HRS ART HIST. PROJ	**10** Psych. 101 = 8-9am / Hist. 201 12-140pm / 1 HR PSYCH. EXAM / 2 HRS HIST PAPER / 1 HR ENG. PAPER	**11** Eng 102=10-12pm / Art Hist. 100 = 1-230pm / 1 HR HIST. EXAM / 1 HR ENG. PAPER	**12** Psych. 101 = 8-9am / Hist. 201 12-140pm / PSYCH EXAM/ 7 HRS STUDY TIME	**13** 1 HR HIST. EXAM	16 HRS 45 MINS
14 2 HRS HIST. EXAM / 1 HR ENG. PAPER / 2 HRS ART HIST. PROJ	**15** Psych. 101 = 8-9am / Hist. 201 12-140pm / 1 HR HIST. EXAM / 2 HRS ART HIST. PROJ	**16** Eng 102=10-12pm / Art Hist. 100 = 1-230pm	**17** Psych. 101 = 8-9am / Hist. 201 12-140pm / 1 HR ART HIST. PROJ / 5 PG HIST. PAPER DUE/ 5 HRS STUDY TIME	**18** Eng 102=10-12pm / Art Hist. 100 = 1-230pm / 1 HR HIST. EXAM / 45 MINS ART HIST. PROJ	**19** Psych. 101 = 8-9am / Hist. 201 12-140pm	**20**	10 HRS 45 MINS
21 2 HRS HIST.EXAM / 3 HRS ART HIST. PROJ	**22** Psych. 101 = 8-9am / Hist. 201 12-140pm / 1 HR HIST. EXAM / 45 MINS ART HIST. PROJ	**23** Eng 102=10-12pm / Art Hist. 100 = 1-230pm / 1 HR PSYCH. QUIZ / 1 HR ART HIST. PROJ	**24** Psych. 101 = 8-9am / Hist. 201 12-140pm / 1 HR PSYCH. QUIZ / HIST. EXAM/ 8 HRS STUDY TIME	**25** Eng 102=10-12pm / Art Hist. 100 = 1-230pm / 1 HR HIST.QUIZ / 10 PG ENG. PAPER DUE/ 5 HRS STUDY TIME	**26** Psych. 101 = 8-9am / Hist. 201 12-140pm	**27**	10 HRS 45 MINS
28 1 HR HIST. QUIZ	**29** Psych. 101 = 8-9am / Hist. 201 12-140pm / 1 HR ART HIST. PROJ / PSYCH. QUIZ/ 2 HRS STUDY TIME	**30** Eng 102=10-12pm / Art Hist. 100 = 1-230pm / HIST. QUIZ/ 2 HRS STUDY TIME	**31** Psych. 101 = 8-9am / Hist. 201 12-140pm / ART HIST. PROJ. DUE/ 20 HRS STUDY TIME				2 HRS SO FAR

To complete all of your assignments on time, and stay ahead during the semester, download the Master Schedule template from the book's website **www.mydebtfreecollege.com/resources**

Your schedule may or may not be as intense as this example. This is a suggestive template, because this calendar only highlights major assignments and is based upon each student keeping up with class reading, group meetings, etc., which are things that you can just add to the calendar. You will have other responsibilities like work, social and/or organizational commitments etc., but sticking to an assignment schedule will help you master your overall schedule. You can see that in using this calendar, there is still a lot of time left in the week to have fun and hang out. Don't forget to add in time to make connections with people who can get you money for school, research and apply for scholarships, etc. Did you notice that there wasn't a lot of studying on Fridays and Saturdays?

Day-to-day activities change. Even though you may think that you can plan your schedule, it will make it hard for you to adapt when unexpected events occur. That is why we have only filled in the amount of time you need to study during a day for each assignment. Even in a single day unexpected things can pop up and your schedule may have to change. You can adjust these occurrences by turning a one-hour study block into two thirty-minute intervals to fit your changing schedule. When you get your schedule for work, organizational meetings, etc., you will be able to fill them in because they are subject to change, unlike your class times which are constant.

To actively use this calendar, you may sync it with your electronic calendar. Attach it to an application like Evernote that can keep your master schedule synced on all of your devices (laptop, phone, desktop), put it on a note card or in your binder. The important thing is to have your master schedule where you can see what you must do each day in order to stay ahead during the semester. There are 168 hours in a week. If you spend eight hours a day sleeping, there are still 112 workable hours left for you to master your schedule.

Here are a few extra tips to help you master your schedule:

- The earlier in the day that you take classes, the more time you have for yourself and for studying.
- Build your schedule around classes so that you can avoid missing classes or leaving early.
- If you have to build your schedule around your life outside of school, make sure you take a manageable amount of credit hours. Take courses during the times that you are absolutely certain that you can attend in order to avoid missing classes or having to leave early or arrive late.
- Be careful to take only the number of courses that you can handle. If you take courses that you don't think you can handle, withdraw before the deadline in order not to receive a "W" (Withdrawal) on your transcript. Avoid having "W's" on your transcript.
- Pay attention in class and set GPA goals.
- Don't be afraid to work with your classmates; they may have strategies that can assist you with time management.
- Create your own study rhythm. I created my own by mixing my basketball coach's strategy with one of my mentor's schedule.
- Balance school and personal life. Both are equally important.
- Avoid switching majors too many times. Many graduates work in fields other than the one in which they received their degree.
- Do not procrastinate until the night before an assignment is due. It is best to complete assignments before the due dates rather than being under pressure of cramming or scrambling to get things turned in.
- Finishing projects or papers.

- Early completion allows time for a low-pressure review of notes and test material.

- It is important to find out which classes are offered during each semester and which classes you do not have to take consecutively. Some classes may only be offered one semester each year. However, before you can take that course, you may have to take the prerequisite. A prerequisite is a course that you must complete before enrolling in a more advanced course. If your academic advisor is uncertain when a class is offered, ask the professor who normally teaches the course. Being aware of prerequisites and when classes are offered is essential in mastering your schedule. Each semester must be planned strategically.

- Most colleges do not allow students to take courses in their majors at other institutions. Take as many general education courses away from your home institution to possibly save money.

Author's Experiences and Opinions:

- *In order to master my college schedule, I was strategic. My college assigned me sixteen credit hours my first semester and expected me to take twelve credit hours the next. After researching that it took 123 credit hours to graduate with a bachelor's degree, I decided I would just take around the same amount they originally assigned me every semester. I knew that a student only had to take twelve credit hours to be full-time but I'm not one to take the easy way out, so I challenged myself. At the end of my first semester, I noticed that there were long lines to get registered for classes and to meet with academic advisors to figure out what classes a student needed to take.*

To avoid these lines in the future, I had to be resourceful, so I figured out that my course catalog listed all of the courses I need to take in order to graduate, and I wrote them down by class level and in which semester that I would take them. When the registration period ended, I consulted with my academic advisor and we forecasted my schedule for the duration of my matriculation (Strategy #3 Building Relationships). As a result I knew what courses I would take each year. All that I had to do was pick class times that were available. There were some semesters that I would have to adjust because class times or course availability changed. But for the most part, the same classes were taught during the same semester each year.

Schedule forecasting and taking more than twelve credit hours per semester helped me to get an entire semester ahead of my graduating class. Being a semester ahead helped immensely when I decided to work toward a second degree during my fourth year.

- *The number of credit hours that it takes to obtain a degree varies by major and institution. For my Bachelor's degrees I had to have over 123 hours because I earned two degrees. I actually ended up graduating with 178 hours. But for a student who needs only 123 credit hours to graduate, taking fifteen credit hours per semester for eight semesters (four years) will grant them 120 credit hours. Which means that they will be short on credits and can't graduate in four years. A student would have to take more than fifteen credit hours during one semester or take a summer or winter course. Make sure that you do your schedule forecasting so that you can graduate on time.*

- *When it came to studying for classes I would take all of my syllabi from each professor and put them together to create an assignment schedule. Then I would either estimate out how long it would take me to complete an assignment or ask my professor how long they thought it would take a student to finish and submit a quality assignment. Then I would write it down on my master schedule how much work each assignment required and work on each assignment according to my calendar. This proved to be easier and less stressful than cramming days before assignments were due. My assignment schedule and master schedule also allowed me to plan my evening and weekends. I worked hard to make sure not to have afternoon classes so that I could study early and hang out later. I didn't figure these two strategies out until after I was in college a few years. Schedule forecasting was helpful for me because it allowed me to have flexibility by knowing how many hours I needed to spend on a subject per day.*

- *Two study and social balance strategies that I learned along my journey were to study five days per week and make sure to finish my classes early in the day. My high school basketball coach told our entire basketball team after practice that he only studied from Sunday through Thursday during college so that he could hang out on Fridays and Saturdays. After hearing his story, I decided that I would follow this strategy.*

  In theory, not studying on Friday and Saturday nights seemed perfect, but when I actually got to college I found out that there were some Fridays and Saturdays that I had to buckle down and study to either get ahead or continue maintaining my grade point average. I had learned to finish my classes early in the day from one of my mentors at the Continentals of Omega Boys & Girls Club. For the most part, I was able to finish my courses early every semester, but there were some semesters when certain classes were only offered later in the evening, and I had to take them.

- *My study rhythm kept me ahead and when I had to, I studied at night. Everyone's rhythm will be different because everyone has different responsibilities in college that include work, athletics, volunteering, campus organizational commitments, etc. I encourage you to use the tools in this chapter to create your own study rhythm.*

  Hanging out, partying, emergencies, and responsibility are all going to happen, but when I handled my academics before anything extra-curricular, the consequences were minimal and I didn't have to subconsciously say to myself, "I should be at home or in the library working on an assignment right now." A clear conscience goes hand-in-hand with enjoying oneself.

- *You can get ahead of your graduating class by taking a fifteen or more credit hours over multiple semesters.*

- *When I was considering earning a second degree, I went to the academic advisor in the school of business to discuss the necessary requirements to complete both degrees. By the time I enrolled, the math requirements to receive a degree from the school of business had changed. The academic advisor told me that I must take the new math class. When I returned for our second conversation, I had my course catalog, which stated that any degree I obtained was to be awarded under the established curriculum at the time I enrolled my freshman year. This meant that I did not have to take the new math class because it was not a part of the curriculum when I enrolled at CAU as a freshman.*

With that issue out of the way, I also noticed that my second major required a certain number of elective courses to be completed. I asked her if the electives and some of the classes that I had taken as a result of my first degree could be used, which proved to be better than my taking elective courses again. Permission for my former electives and some classes in my first major of Fashion Design/Merchandising was granted and circumstances worked out where I would only have to spend one extra year in school. I knew the statute of limitations on my school's curriculum (using my course catalog) and had planned out how I could obtain my second degree without re-taking courses before signing up. I left the meeting with the academic advisor with the results that I desired.

THE TWO-FOR-TWO STRATEGY

Not everyone who attends a four-year college or university starts out there. If you have not excelled at the high school level (Strategy 1), or cannot decide which college/university you would like to attend, you should consider attending a community college to complete your general education requirements. The good thing about attending a community college is that they are cheaper than four-year colleges or universities.

While it's sometimes the road less traveled by college students, there are advantages to attending a community college:

- It is affordable; costing just a fraction of the price you would pay to attend a four-year college or university *(See Tables 2 and 3 at the end of this strategy)*.
- Financial aid is available to those who qualify.
- You can live at home and work toward an Associate's degree before transferring to a four-year college to earn a Bachelor's degree.
- You will have an opportunity to improve your GPA, which will enhance your chances of getting into the four-year college of your choice.
- You will have enough time to research and apply for scholarships that may cover the cost of your last two years at the four-year college or university of your choice.

Community college is usually affordable to the extent that you can pay for your class expenses out of pocket. Financial aid is also available at community colleges. For example, if a student at a four-year college has $5,000 in grant money, he or she may need an additional $20-25,000 to cover school expenses. With that same $5,000 in grants, a student may be able to cover all of his or her school expenses for the year at a community college.

While pursuing the Two-for-Two strategy, you should always be in contact with your academic advisor to ensure that you are taking the correct courses and staying on track toward earning your Associate's degree. Also, confirm with the four-year college you wish to transfer to that **1)** all courses you take while enrolled in community college are transferrable and **2)** you're taking the correct required courses for your area of study.

It is important to know how many credit hours are transferable so that you do not take more classes than necessary. You do not want to take classes for two years and only be able to transfer partial credits to your four-year college/university.

Being certain that your credits are transferable is your responsibility. Get all commitments, permissions, agreements, etc., in writing and keep them in a special file until your graduation. Use your additional two years to accumulate the resources that you will need to cover tuition and expenses at your four-year college or university. The goal is to be debt-free. Attending a community college at a fraction of the cost of a four-year college is a great starting point.

This is one of the best strategies for achieving a debt-free college education. If my sole objective was the cost of my education, I would have considered enrolling for my first two years at a community college.

Author's Experiences & Opinions

- *During my sophomore year, as the school year wound down, I decided that I wanted to take a graphics class in the fall to further enhance the clothing line I had founded. I also decided that it would be smart to take one of my core classes (economics) to get ahead since I would be in school during the summer anyway. Summer school courses at Clark Atlanta University were $365 per credit hour and both classes were three credit hours, so that was $1,095 per course ($2,190 total). I knew that I did not want to take out a loan so I had to figure out a cheaper solution. I did some research and found classes for $12 per credit hour $36 per course ($72 total) at two different community colleges at home in California. After finding my classes, I checked to make sure that they were equivalent to those offered at CAU. I went to my academic department and the Registrar's office and obtained approval for my courses at the community college so that the credits I earned would transfer to CAU.*

One class was in the morning and the other was at night. For the majority of that summer, I went to class early in the morning, worked in the afternoon, and went back to class at night.

The two colleges are about an hour apart and I worked and lived in a city between both of them, but in order to avoid student loans and take that graphic design class to help my business, I was willing to do anything.

Let's do the math for the difference in course prices:

Clark Atlanta University: $365 X 3 credit hours = $1,095 per course X 2 = $2,190

California Community College: $12 X 3 credit hours = $36 per course X 2 = $72

The difference in price for one course at community college *versus at CAU was $1,059! I took two courses that summer and saved $2,118. After doing the math, I took as many courses at California community colleges as I could.*

This table highlights the estimated cost of public college in the U.S.

*In dollars. Estimated, for the entire academic year ending in year shown. Figures are average charges per full-time equivalent student. Room and board are based on full-time students]

PUBLIC INSTITUTIONS

ACADEMIC YEAR	TUITION & REQUIRED FEES			BOARD RATES			DORMITORY RATES			TOTALS		
	2-YEAR COLLEGES	4-YEAR UNIVERSITIES	OTHER 4-YEAR SCHOOLS	2-YEAR COLLEGES	4-YEAR UNIVERSITIES	OTHER 4-YEAR SCHOOLS	2-YEAR COLLEGES	4-YEAR UNIVERSITIES	OTHER 4-YEAR SCHOOLS	2-YEAR COLLEGES	4-YEAR UNIVERSITIES	OTHER 4-YEAR SCHOOLS
2010	$2,285	$8,123	$5,964	$2,574	$4,018	$3,578	$2,845	$4,571	$4,561	$7,704	$16,712	$14,103
2011	$2,422	$8,610	$6,322	$2,728	$4,259	$3,793	$3,016	$4,845	$4,835	$8,166	$17,715	$14,949
2012	$2,567	$9,127	$6,701	$2,892	$4,515	$4,020	$3,197	$5,136	$5,125	$8,656	$18,778	$15,846
2013	$2,721	$9,675	$7,103	$3,066	$4,786	$4,261	$3,388	$5,444	$5,432	$9,176	$19,904	$16,797
2014	$2,885	$10,255	$7,529	$3,250	$5,073	$4,517	$3,592	$5,771	$5,758	$9,726	$21,099	$17,805
2015	$3,058	$10,870	$7,981	$3,445	$5,377	$4,788	$3,807	$6,117	$6,104	$10,310	$22,364	$18,873
2016	$3,241	$11,523	$8,460	$3,651	$5,700	$5,075	$4,036	$6,484	$6,470	$10,928	$23,706	$20,005
2017	$3,436	$12,214	$8,968	$3,870	$6,042	$5,380	$4,278	$6,873	$6,858	$11,584	$25,129	$21,206
2018	$3,642	$12,947	$9,506	$4,103	$6,404	$5,703	$4,534	$7,285	$7,270	$12,279	$26,636	$22,478
2019	$3,860	$13,724	$10,076	$4,349	$6,788	$6,045	$4,807	$7,723	$7,706	$13,016	$28,235	$23,827
2020	$4,092	$14,547	$10,681	$4,610	$7,196	$6,408	$5,095	$8,186	$8,168	$13,797	$29,929	$25,256

Table 2 Cost of Education Chart – (available for download at www.mydebtfreecollege.com/resources)

For public institutions, data is for in-state students. Beginning 1990, rates reflect 20 meals per week, rather than meals served 7 days a week. Source: U.S. National Center for Education Statistics, Digest of Education Statistics, annual.
See also http://www.census.gov/compendia/statab/2012/tables/12s0293.pdf or <http://www.nces.ed.gov/programs/digest/>.
*Extended data beyond the year 2010 has been calculated using a 6% annual increase.

This table highlights the estimated cost of private college in the U.S

In dollars. Estimated, for the entire academic year ending in year shown. Figures are average charges per full-time equivalent student. Room and board are based on full-time students]

PRIVATE INSTITUTIONS

ACADEMIC YEAR	TUITION & REQUIRED FEES			BOARD RATES			DORMITORY RATES			TOTALS		
	2-YEAR COLLEGES	4-YEAR UNIVERSITIES	OTHER 4-YEAR SCHOOLS	2-YEAR COLLEGES	4-YEAR UNIVERSITIES	OTHER 4-YEAR SCHOOLS	2-YEAR COLLEGES	4-YEAR UNIVERSITIES	OTHER 4-YEAR SCHOOLS	2-YEAR COLLEGES	4-YEAR UNIVERSITIES	OTHER 4-YEAR SCHOOLS
2010	$14,876	$33,315	$21,244	$4,390	$4,765	$4,205	$5,217	$6,539	$4,897	$24,483	$44,619	$30,346
2011	$15,619	$34,981	$22,306	$4,609	$5,003	$4,415	$5,477	$6,865	$5,141	$25,952	$47,296	$32,167
2012	$16,715	$37,433	$23,870	$4,933	$5,354	$4,725	$5,862	$7,347	$5,502	$27,509	$50,134	$34,097
2013	$17,718	$39,679	$25,302	$5,229	$5,675	$5,008	$6,214	$7,788	$5,832	$29,160	$53,142	$36,143
2014	$18,781	$42,059	$26,820	$5,542	$6,016	$5,309	$6,586	$8,255	$6,182	$30,909	$56,330	$38,311
2015	$19,907	$44,583	$28,429	$5,875	$6,377	$5,627	$6,982	$8,751	$6,553	$32,764	$59,710	$40,610
2016	$21,102	$47,258	$30,135	$6,227	$6,759	$5,965	$7,400	$9,276	$6,946	$34,730	$63,293	$43,046
2017	$22,368	$50,093	$31,943	$6,601	$7,165	$6,323	$7,844	$9,832	$7,363	$36,813	$67,090	$45,629
2018	$23,710	$53,099	$33,860	$6,997	$7,595	$6,702	$8,315	$10,422	$7,805	$39,022	$71,116	$48,367
2019	$25,133	$56,285	$35,891	$7,417	$8,050	$7,104	$8,814	$11,048	$8,273	$41,364	$75,383	$51,269
2020	$26,641	$59,662	$38,045	$7,862	$8,533	$7,531	$9,343	$11,710	$8,770	$43,845	$79,906	$54,345

Table 3 Cost of Education Chart – (available for download at www.mydebtfreecollege.com/resources)

For public institutions, data is for in-state students. Beginning 1990, rates reflect 20 meals per week, rather than meals served 7 days a week. Source: U.S. National Center for Education Statistics, Digest of Education Statistics, annual.
See also http://www.census.gov/compendia/statab/2012/tables/12s0293.pdf or <http://www.nces.ed.gov/programs/digest/>.
*Extended data beyond the year 2010 has been calculated using a 6% annual increase.

9

FIND EMPLOYMENT

Many students work while enrolled in college to cover the costs of tuition, books, and any other expenses. When using this strategy, the balance between work, studying, and social time is vital to your college success. Ideally, you will want to be in a position where you are working because you want to, not because you must. It is a great feeling to be able to focus solely on school and enjoy the full college experience. However, achieving the goal of a debt-free college education requires that you must do whatever it takes.

When looking for employment, it is best to begin researching the jobs or work-study programs your campus offers. This strategy will help you to avoid commuting to and from work. The campus' career center and bulletin boards are good sources for job opportunities.

Once you find a job, you don't want to compromise your GPA or class work by working too much. If you do, you can risk losing certain scholarships, eligibility of certain scholarships, or being placed on academic probation. To avoid this, work study programs offer flexible schedules and federal law states that you can work up to twenty hours per week. If you must work, my suggestions are to work nights, after class, or on weekends when classes are not in session.

Another option to think about is working multiple jobs during the summer, winter, and holiday breaks so that you can devote more time to class work during the school year. **Obtaining an off-campus job during the semester should be your last resort!** If you do work off campus you'll be spending valuable money on transportation that you could be putting toward school expenses.

Other on-campus job options include working as a teacher's or librarian's assistant, joining your student government association (SGA), working in the cafeteria, or patrolling the campus grounds or facilities management.

One on-campus job to also consider is becoming a resident assistant (RA). This job often provides room and board (a place to live and a meal plan) in exchange for your supervision of student residents, providing cultural dormitory programs, and monitoring your residence hall.

Author's Experiences and Opinions:

- *Some summers I worked and took classes. During other breaks, I worked full time. To avoid having to work during the school year, I saved my summer earnings to use for school expenses. In addition to working, I sold dinners in my neighborhood to raise money. Without those creative strategies and fundraisers, I would now have student loan debt. So be creative when working in the summer. People are more supportive than you think*

- *I had various jobs on campus throughout my college years; some were work-study and some were not. I was always honest with my employers, letting them know that school was my number one priority. As a result in most situations, I was able to negotiate my schedule.*

- *As a work-study student in my freshman year, I watched the front desk and checked students into my freshman dormitory.*

- *I was an RA during my sophomore year and it proved to be a very enlightening experience. I learned a lot from the residents and about myself. I actually learned to dance the salsa as a result of my producing a dance program with my all-male dormitory and an all-female dormitory. As an RA, I received on-campus housing and a meal plan in exchange for my services.*

- *Another year, I worked as a work-study student being an office assistant in the fashion department.*

- *One of my other jobs during my college matriculation was to go into different offices and survey/rate the way that staff treated students and report my findings to the Retention Services office.*

- *Federal law states that twenty hours is the maximum number of hours a work-study student can work per week. This meant that I had to balance work, schoolwork and my social life.*

Playing basketball as well as being a designer made it difficult at first, but I selected work-study jobs where I was able to do schoolwork while on duty. This worked out well.

- *Try to find a job where you can complete class assignments while working.*

10

BE FINANCIALLY SMART

Though college can be the best part of your life, it can also be one of the most difficult financial times of your life. While achieving your debt-free college education, budgeting will be an absolutely necessary skill. DO NOT, and I repeat, DO NOT TAKE ANY CREDIT CARDS UNLESS YOU ABSOLUTELY MUST. If managed correctly, credit cards can help establish good credit. However, you must be responsible. Credit cards are not free money and the balance you place on them should be looked at as debt that needs to be paid as soon as possible. Do not obtain credit cards because you want to buy clothes, a car, a vacation, or have some fun. Trust me: building credit in college is not a requirement. Save the luxuries until after you have obtained your debt-free college education.

Before we go any further in this strategy let's understand the following:

An **asset** is something that makes a profit periodically or when it is sold.

A **liability** is something that takes money away from you or loses money when it is sold.

ASSETS	LIABILITIES
Cash	Mortgage
House	Clothing
Rental Property	Car
Stocks, bonds & mutual funds	Student loans (other loans)
Retirement accounts (401(k) and IRAs)	Credit card debt

Do not spend all your money on liabilities. Use your money wisely. Don't just spend it to be spending. You must budget for your expenses—necessities, fun, and other areas of your life. When budgeting, be as specific as possible. Should you need to increase your income, be creative and save change when you break a dollar, or sell dinners door-to-door like I did. If you need to save money, be disciplined.

Do not purchase a new car, live beyond your means, or obtain a credit card unless you absolutely need one. If you are on a limited budget, you should not be eating out at restaurants every day, buying new clothes, or going on expensive dates. You must be resourceful and find whatever free or inexpensive (cheap) options are available. Remember the people who are signing starving college students up for credit cards in exchange for free gifts are not there to help you. They are there to make money and credit card companies make the most money as a result of missed payments, not to mention the administrative fees after accounts have gone into collections.

In college, you will see that other students receive refund checks from their college loans. Instead of giving the money back to student loan lenders, often they will spend it on liabilities such as cars, clothes, or other purchases that seem good at the moment. Remember that any amount of money borrowed for college must start being repaid six to nine months after graduation. By being financially smart, you may feel like you don't have the same things other students have at times, but believe me, they will wish they had your freedom when their student loans kick in, especially if they have difficulty finding a job after college. If you can master the skill of budgeting to gain a debt-free college education this skill will assist you later on in life. A financially smart mindset is priceless and is very helpful for purchases of all sizes.

By staying debt-free in college, you have a higher chance of having a favorable credit score post-college, which can help you get the best interest rates on purchases that rely on your credit score. However, a debt-free college education does not always equal a favorable credit score. A great credit score depends on handling your payments responsibly. Being financially smart is not only an important lesson in being a debt-free college student; it is also a critical factor in living a debt-free life.

When you sign up on the book's website, **www.mydebtfreecollege.com**, you will receive access to a free video tutorial that teaches you how to budget for each semester of college. You will also receive a free Microsoft excel semester budgeting spreadsheet download that will calculate all of your college financial information. This spreadsheet will help you see where you are in terms of needing more or less scholarship money. I used a semester budgeting worksheet every year that I was in college. It assisted me in achieving my debt-free college education. On the following page is an example of the semester budgeting worksheet.

SEMESTER BUDGETING WORKSHEET

SEMESTER _____
YEAR _____

INCOME	ESTIMATED	ACTUAL
GRANTS	$	$
SCHOLARSHIPS	$	$
JOB (SALARY)	$	$
PARENTS	$	$
SAVINGS	$	$
WORK-STUDY	$	$
PUBLIC BENEFITS	$	$
SPOUSE SUPPORT	$	$
OTHER	$	$
INCOME TOTALS	$	$

ACADEMIC EXPENSES	ESTIMATED	ACTUAL
TUITION	$	$
FEES	$	$
BOOKS	$	$
SUPPLIES	$	$
OTHER	$	$
ACADEMIC EXPENSE TOTALS	$	$

LIVING EXPENSES	ESTIMATED	ACTUAL
ROOM / RENT	$	$
BOARD/ MEALS	$	$
UTILITIES (WATER, GAS, ELECTRIC, TRASH & SEWAGE)	$	$
PHONE	$	$
TV (CABLE, DVDs, ETC)	$	$
TOILETRIES	$	$
LAUNDRY / DRY CLEANING	$	$
CREDIT CARD PAYMENTS	$	$
TRANSPORTATION (GAS, PARKING, INSURANCE, ETC)	$	$
OTHER	$	$
LIVING EXPENSE TOTALS	$	$

PERSONAL EXPENSES	ESTIMATED	ACTUAL
BARBER/ SALON	$	$
ENTERTAINMENT (MOVIES, MUSIC, EVENTS, DINING OUT)	$	$
CLOTHING	$	$
TRAVEL	$	$
OTHER	$	$
PERSONAL EXPENSE TOTALS	$	$

		ESTIMATED	ACTUAL
INCOME	**A.** TOTAL INCOME	$	$
EXPENSES	TOTAL ACADEMIC EXPENSES (FROM ABOVE)	$	$
	TOTAL LIVING EXPENSES (FROM ABOVE)	$	$
	TOTAL PERSONAL EXPENSES (FROM ABOVE)	$	$
	B. TOTAL EXPENSES	$	$

START WITH LINE A THEN SUBTRACT LINE B
TO GET YOUR NET INCOME
(INCOME MINUS EXPENSES EQUALS MONEY FOR SAVINGS)

$ $

Author's Experiences and Opinions:

- *At the end of each semester I estimated my income for the following semester. During my junior year I estimated my income for my senior year. After creating a budget, I thought about and researched where I could save money. I noticed that the cost to stay in on-campus housing was close to $6,000 for nine months. On-campus housing was fun and many of my friends lived in the dorms, but I sought out a less expensive opportunity.*

  One of my good friends from California lived with students in a boarding house within walking distance of campus for $300 per month, all utilities included ($3,600 a year). When I did the math, I noticed that I could save almost $2,400, avoid taking out a loan for school, and avoid moving/storage expenses at the end of each break in the academic year.

  I moved into the boarding house and saved more than just $2,400: because the $2,400 that I would have borrowed to pay for on-campus housing would have had to be repaid with interest. Budgeting for each academic year was a consistent method that I used to save and avoid loans.

Remember there is no one right way to achieve the debt-free college goal. I used a combination of these strategies and today I enjoy post-college freedom on a totally different level than those who financed college with student loans. Start creating your plan NOW and use the ten strategies and other resources in this book to earn your debt-free college education.

QUICK TIPS

When applying to college, remember to use these quick tips. They can save you tons of time and money in the future!

- Consider cost as a primary factor.
- Apply to multiple schools and weigh all of the financial aid packages; try to negotiate for a better financial aid package if necessary by telling financial aid officers what other schools are offering you.
- Look at each of your potential schools' graduation rates, and the average length of attendance. Is it 4, 5, or 6 years?
- Consider financial aid safety schools (schools that you can attend and pay for without financial aid).
- Don't go to for-profit colleges. They can shut down by filing bankruptcy and leave you with student loan debt and no degree.

More tips:

- Get informed and be proactive about the financial future of college and your life.
- The amount of United States student loan debt is now over one trillion dollars; don't allow yourself to be included in this total.
- Admissions officers are like sales representatives for their respective colleges. Their job is to attract the biggest student body and get low acceptance rates to boost their college's rankings.
- A financial aid officer's job is to make sure that students pay their tuition and fees. Unless you establish a relationship with some of them, you'll need to be aware of your financial standing as a student. Be focused and know what's going on with your financial aid account at all times.
- Always try to renegotiate your financial aid packages to receive the as much free money as possible.
- Ask family and friends to invest in your education.

- All financial aid information that you receive, as well as checks and balance statements, need to be in writing and kept stored in a safe place until after you graduate.
- Check with your high school counselor and the college/university you would like to attend. Their Continuing Studies or Registrar's office will have more information on the availability of tests.
- The option to test out of classes is sometimes offered when you get to college. You should actively look for and try to take advantage of opportunities to test out of classes because it can free up your time to earn money and research scholarships for the current or upcoming academic year.
- Remember to build strong relationships with people who are able to help you continue your education.
- If you receive a large scholarship in your financial award letter, always ask your financial aid advisor to reduce your loans so that you can show a need to receive the entire scholarship. Sometimes scholarship amounts are reduced because a student is offered a lot of money in student loans.
- Actively pursue scholarships, work-study, grants, and other types of financial aid that do not require you to pay the money back.
- Work hard for your debt-free college education by applying for scholarships and grants and you'll reap the rewards later.
- There are over two million other students applying for the same federal college funding as you. Be pro-active instead of reactive. Don't wait until after January to start gathering your documents for your FAFSA application.
- Don't switch majors or transfer to another four-year college. These changes may invite unforeseen financial issues. Keep in mind that many people have careers outside of their majors.
- Find out which courses can be taken at community colleges. Take those courses during the summer or winter breaks either back home, or near your school. It is a cheaper way to help pay for four years of college.
- If you must work, try to work part-time during the school year and full-time during the summer to earn money for

college. Working during these times will allow you to have time to focus on your courses and course work.

SCHOLARSHIPS

NAVIGATING THE SCHOLARSHIP SECTION

Steps to Finding and securing a scholarship

1. Read about and highlight each scholarship you qualify for.
2. Go to each scholarship's website to retrieve the application.
3. Gather the required application materials and submit them with your application. (Many of the scholarships listed can be completed and submitted online. Before mailing materials check the scholarships website for up to date information.

The following scholarship information is subject to change at the scholarship sponsors discretion.

- Scholarship contact person
- Websites, email addresses and links. Companies are improving and restructuring frequently. If a scholarship link is no longer working, try typing the name of the scholarship in a search engine (e.g. like Google or Internet Explorer.)
- Scholarship deadline dates change every year. Use the dates on the scholarship list as a guideline to meet the deadline. Always check the scholarships website for the most up to date application deadline.

How to find the scholarship section on websites:

- Look for keywords in the headers such as programs, scholarships, awards or type the word scholarship in the website's search box.

How to find the most up-to-date information on a scholarship website:

Check the websites "about pages", Frequently Asked Questions (FAQ) pages, "contact us" pages or call them directly to ask any questions that you may have.

All of the most up to date information for the scholarships in this section was accurate as of the production date however it is subject to change. To always have the most current information for any scholarship you should always look at the scholarships website or call the scholarship sponsor.

*This section is available to give you a head start in gaining free money for college.

HIGH SCHOOL SCHOLARSHIPS

* While the author has done his best to make sure all information in this section is accurate and up to date, all scholarship deadlines are subject to change at the sponsor's discretion. You should double-check all deadlines on each scholarships website for the most up to date information.

( ) Parenthesis indicate the quantity of scholarships available

AFA Teens for Alzheimer's Awareness College Scholarship

Overview: As more and more families across America are affected by Alzheimer's disease, many teenagers as well are becoming aware of this heartbreaking brain disease—from personal experiences in their own families, watching friends and neighbors, or involvement in community service. Recognizing this, the Alzheimer's Foundation of America (AFA), a national non-profit organization, has created a division specifically for teens, AFA Teens. Its goals include raising awareness among teenagers and the public about Alzheimer's disease and related dementias; providing education, counseling, and support to young family members; enabling teens to share feelings with other teens and experts; and referring teens and their family members to supportive services. In a further effort to provide an outlet for teenagers to express their thoughts about Alzheimer's disease and to engage the younger generation in this cause, AFA is pleased to offer the AFA Teens for Alzheimer's Awareness College Scholarship.

Eligibility Requirements: Applicants must have United States citizenship or permanent residency, plan to enter an accredited four-year college/university within 12 months of the scholarship deadline, be currently enrolled in a public, independent, parochial, military, home-school or other high school in the United States (if not currently enrolled, please explain extenuating circumstances), and submit all required materials by the application deadline. In order to be named winner or runners-up and to process the scholarship award, the winner and runners-up will be required to supply his or her Social Security number, and submit proof of high school enrollment (i.e., official transcript) and U.S. citizenship (passport, birth certificate; driver's license is not acceptable); and he or she subsequently must provide official documentation of registration from the college/university that he or she is attending in the following fall or spring in order to receive the scholarship monies.

Amount: (1) annual $5,000 scholarship will be awarded to one deserving college-bound student (1) $500 (1) $250 scholarships to 1st and 2nd runners up, respectively.

Deadline: February 15th

Address: Alzheimer's Foundation of America
322 Eighth Ave., 7th Fl. New York, NY 10001
Attn: AFA Teens College Scholarship

Contact: info@afateens.org

Telephone: Jessie McHessey at 1-866-232-8484

Website: http://www.afateens.org/about_new.html

Al Neuharth Free Spirit Scholarship and Journalism Conference

Overview: The annual Al Neuharth Free Spirit Scholarship and Journalism Conference program awards $1,000 college scholarships to rising high school seniors who are interested in pursuing a career in journalism and who demonstrate qualities of "free spirit." Students will come to Washington, D.C., July 1 of the applying year to receive their awards and participate in an all-expenses-paid journalism conference at the Newseum, located at 555 Pennsylvania Ave., N.W. This program began in 1999 and is funded by the Freedom Forum to honor Al Neuharth, the founder of *USA TODAY*, Newseum and the Freedom Forum. The scholarships and conference are designed to inspire and encourage students to pursue journalism.

Eligibility Requirements: Applicants must be high school juniors; committed to pursuing a career in journalism; demonstrating; qualities of a "free spirit" and be available to attend the conference in July located in Washington D.C.

Amount: $1,000
Deadline: February 15th
Address: Free Spirit Organization
                Attn: Scholarship Committee
                555 Pennsylvania Ave., N.W.
                Washington, DC 20001
Contact: freespirit@freedomforum.org
Telephone: Karen Catone at (202) 292-6271
Website: http://www.freedomforum.org/freespirit/

Anne Frank Outstanding Scholarship Award

Overview: In honor of the anniversary of Anne Frank's birthday on June 12, the Anne Frank Center USA celebrates with the annual Spirit of Anne Frank Awards for citizens, educators and graduating high school students.

Eligibility Requirements: Applicants must be graduating high school seniors who are community leaders and have been accepted to a four-year college. The award recognizes students who exemplify the commitment, ideals and courage that Anne Frank represents today. Examples of such activities include Acting as spokespersons for tolerance; on a daily basis, having the courage to be bridge builders and peacemakers; Creating in programs that address intolerance, violence prevention and conflict resolution; Standing up against intolerance by leading or participating in community-based organizations. Applicants are required to write a 1,000-word essay describing contributions they have made to their community and how Anne Frank inspires their goals. The essay should relate a single personal experience that demonstrates a commitment to social justice. We strongly recommend that applicants read "Anne Frank: The Diary of a Young Girl" and include in their essay how themes from the diary relate to their own life experience. Applicants are also required to provide two letters of recommendation on letterhead from supporting sponsors who are personally familiar with the applicant's contributions but are not parents or family members. All application materials must be postmarked by January 31st. The winner will be announced on March 28. Applicable Majors:

All Fields of Study.

Amount:	$10,000
Deadline:	January 31st
Address:	Anne Frank Center, USA
	44 Park Place New York, NY 10007
Contact:	mmcneil@annefrank.com
Telephone:	(212) 431-7993 ext. 302
Website:	http://www.annefrank.com

Ashley Marie Easterbrook Scholarship Fund

Overview: Ashley Easterbrook was a very special young lady with a strong interest in helping others. Her volunteer efforts included organizing a benefit for the residents of a battered woman's shelter, organizing Special Olympics events and founding a tutoring program for bilingual students. Five days prior to her high school graduation, Ashley and two friends were killed by a drunk driver. A scholarship fund has been established in Ashley's name to carry on her desire to help others. The non-profit 501(c)(3) fund provides scholarships for students throughout the United States. The fund also assists student organizations and anti-drunk-driving agencies with educational programs.

Eligibility Requirements: Applicant must currently be a high school student (or home schooled) in the United States, graduating in the spring of the current year; have a cumulative 4-year Grade Point Average between 3.50 and 3.74 (un-weighted); transcript verifying GPA (as of at least 12/31/11) and students should be attending an accredited 4-year University or College.

Amount:	$1,000
Deadline:	March 31st
Address:	The Foundation for Ashley's Dream
	675 E. Big Beaver Road
	Suite 101
	Troy, MI 48083
Contact:	info@ashleysdream.org

Telephone: (248) 720-0245
Website: http://www.ashleysdream.org/

Battle for the Bands Scholarship

Overview: Music education is under attack! Despite the proven fact that students who participate in music programs have better test scores, lower drug-use rates, lower drop-out rates, more success in college and more involvement in their communities, music and art education programs have their budgets slashed every year. Dosomething.org launched a campaign to help you save music education by sharing a video.

Eligibility Requirements: Each Group member must be a legal resident of the U.S. residing in one of the fifty (50) United States or the District of Columbia or a legal resident of Canada (excluding the province of Quebec) who is between 13 and 25 years old at the time of Submission. Residents of Maine must be 18 years of age or older. Registration includes having a complete and valid postal mailing address (street/city/state or province/zip or postal code) and phone number on file for the Group Captain at the Website in order to be contacted by mail in the event the Group's Submission is selected as Finalist Submission or Winner in the Contest. Employees of DoSomething, Inc., The VH1 Save the Music Foundation, their respective parent companies, subsidiaries, affiliates, divisions, distributors, suppliers, printers, distributors and advertising and judging agencies and the immediate family members (parent, child, sibling, spouse) and persons living in the same household as such employees (whether related or not) are not eligible to participate as part of a Group or win. (See official scholarship rules)

Amount: 1 Overall Grand Prize: $5,000 grant to keep your school music program alive Up to $1,000 per group member. Example: 5 members receive $1,000 each or 20 members receive $500 each.
Deadline: April 26th
Address: Do Something, Inc.
24-32 Union Square East, 4th Floor

New York, NY 10003
Contact: battle@dosomething.org.
Telephone: (212) 254-2390
Website: http://www.dosomething.org/battle

Chair Scholars Foundation: National Scholarship Program for Students with Disabilities

Overview: Available to students in every state in the continental U.S., the Chair Scholars National Scholarship Program provides eligible high school seniors and college freshmen up to $20,000 for tuition to attend the college or university of their choice.

Eligibility Requirements: The student must be physically challenged and may be "chair-confined". The physical challenge must be significant. No minor disability will be considered. Must have verifiable unmet financial need. Must have at least a B average. Must be a high school senior or college freshman. (Sponsor does not fund graduate studies and does not consider applicants over the age of 21, unless he or she is a college freshman.) The applicant must show some form of significant community service or social contribution in the past. Applicants will be considered without regard to gender, race, creed, or religion.

Amount: (15-20) $1,000 to $5,000 awards. Maximum of $20,000 over four years
Deadline: February 28th
Address: Chair Scholars Foundation
16101 Carencia Lane
Odessa, FL 33556-3278
Telephone: (813) 926-0544 or (888) 926-0544
Fax: (813) 920-7661
Website: http://www.chairscholars.org/national.html

Coca-Cola Scholars Program

Overview: Seniors in high schools throughout the United States who meet the eligibility requirements may apply each year for one of 250 four-year, achievement-based scholarships. Approximately 2,200 applicants will be selected as Semi-finalists and notified by mail and email around December 1. Semi-finalists must then complete a secondary application, including essays, official transcripts, and two letters of recommendation. Semi-finalist applications are due by mid-January. Our Program Review Committee will select 250 Finalists to advance to the final interview phase. Notifications are sent mid-February. In April, the 250 Finalists are invited to Atlanta for personal interviews. A National Selection Committee representing outstanding leaders in business, government, education and the arts interviews the Finalists. 50 students are then designated as National Scholars and receive awards of $20,000 for college; 200 students are designated as Regional Scholars and receive awards of $10,000 for college.

Eligibility Requirements: Applicants must be current high school (or home-schooled) seniors attending school in the United States. US Citizens; US Nationals; US Permanent Residents; Temporary Residents (in a legalization program); Refugees; Asylees; Cuban-Haitian Entrants or Humanitarian Paroles; Seniors anticipating completion of a high school diploma during the academic year in which application is made; Seniors planning to pursue a degree at an accredited US postsecondary institution; Seniors carrying a minimum 3.0 GPA at the end of their junior year of high school.

Applicants may not be: Children or grandchildren of employees, officers or owners of Coca-Cola bottling companies, The Coca-Cola Company, Company divisions or subsidiaries.

Amount:	(50) $20,000 & (200) $10,000 awards
Deadline:	October 31st
Address:	Coca-Cola Scholars Foundation, Inc.
	P.O. Box 442
	Atlanta, GA 30301
Contact:	scholars@na.ko.com
Telephone:	1-800-306-2653
Website:	http://www.coca-colascholars.org

Courageous Persuaders Scholarship

Overview: Each year, more than 10,000 young people, ages 16 to 25, die as a result of alcohol use. It is a tragic problem. As early as grade school, kids feel pressure to drink. Sometimes, the courage to say "no" can come from an older kid. In Courageous Persuaders®, high school students create television commercials targeted at middle school students to warn them about the dangers of alcohol use. Students compete for scholarship money and trophies. The grand prize-winning commercial actually airs on TV as a public service announcement. Participants gain valuable experience, are honored in a Hollywood-style awards banquet and, most importantly, have an opportunity to save lives.

The Grand Prize-winning commercial will be broadcast on television and the team that created it will work with Pluto Post Productions, a postproduction facility that provides a final polish, upgrade, or professional mix to the Grand Prize Courageous Persuaders® video. The top four prize-winning teams will receive trophies, award certificates and scholarship money. The total amount of each scholarship will be distributed among the members of the winning teams.

Eligibility Requirements: Applicants must be current high school students and residents of Michigan

Amount:	Grand Prize Courageous Persuaders® Award $3,000, 1st Place Courageous Persuaders® Award $1,500, 2nd Place Courageous Persuaders® Award $1,000, 3rd Place Courageous Persuaders® Award $500
Address:	Courageous Persuaders 900 West Big Beaver Road, Suite 100 Troy MI 48084
Deadline:	February 9th
Contact:	Sandy Herp, sherp@dada.org
Telephone:	(248) 283-5138
Website:	http://www.courageouspersuaders.com/rules.htm

Davidson Fellow Scholarship

Overview: The Davidson Fellows Scholarship awards $50,000, $25,000 and $10,000 scholarships to extraordinary young people, 18 and under, who have completed a significant piece of work. Application categories are Mathematics, Science, Literature, Music, Technology, Philosophy and Outside the Box. Davidson Fellows are honored every year in Washington, D.C. with Congressional meetings and a special reception.

Eligibility Requirements: Applicants must be 18 or younger as of October 4, 2012. Be a U.S. citizen residing in the United States, or a Permanent Resident of the United States residing in the United States, or be stationed overseas due to active U. S. military duty. There is no minimum age for eligibility. The Davidson Institute is looking for students whose projects are at or close to the college graduate level with a depth of knowledge in their particular area of study. This scholarship is not geared toward students at the novice level. Davidson Fellows must be available to attend, with at least one parent or guardian, the awards reception and other recognition events to be held in October of each academic year in Washington, D.C. (Travel expenses and lodging will be provided by the Institute.)

Amount: (1) $50,000 award (1) $25,000 award (1) $10,000 award

Deadline: February 1st

Address: Davidson Institute for Talent Development
9665 Gateway Drive, Suite B
Reno, NV 89521

Contact: info@davidsongifted.org

Telephone: (775) 852-3483 ext. 435

Fax: (775) 852-2184

Website: http://www.davidsongifted.org/fellows/

Davis Memorial Foundation Scholarship

Overview: The Davis Memorial Foundation currently awards each year to individuals who want to further their education. The Foundation gives priority to students who want to attend a trade school, or get a college or university degree that relates to the construction industry. Employees, spouses, and children of roofing industry professionals in particular are encouraged to apply. Awards are based on both academic and personal achievements. Although financial need is not a requirement for the award, the Foundation will consider level of financial need as the final criteria if, in the judgment of the selection committee, candidates are otherwise ranked equally.

Eligibility Requirements: Applicant must meet one of the following requirements: (1) Currently attend a high school, technical trade school, or college or university (graduate or undergraduate) (2) been accepted into a college, university, or trade school (3) be an employee of a roofing professional (4) be a spouse, child (by birth or legal adoption), or step-child of a roofing professional.

Amount:	TBD
Deadline:	April 15th
Contact:	dmf@wsrca.com
Address:	Davis Memorial Foundation
	465 Fairchild Drive, Suite 210
	Mountain View, CA 94043
Telephone:	(650) 938-5405
Fax:	(650) 938-5407
Website	http://www.davisfoundation.org/scholar/ index.htm

Dell Scholars Program

Overview: While many students dream of obtaining a college degree, life sometimes gets in the way, particularly for those dealing with personal responsibilities at home or in their communities. The Dell Scholars program, an initiative of the Michael & Susan Dell Foundation, recognizes students who have overcome significant obstacles to pursue their educations. In turn, these scholars serve as positive role models and change the trajectories for their siblings, friends, and their communities.

Eligibility Requirements: Applicants must participate in a Michael & Susan Dell Foundation approved college readiness program for a minimum of two, of the last three years, of high school; Graduate from an accredited high school this academic year; earn a minimum of a 2.4 GPA; Demonstrate need for financial assistance; Plan to enter a bachelor's degree program at an accredited higher education institution in the fall directly after graduation from high school; Have U.S. citizenship or permanent residency. Dell Scholars are students who demonstrate their desire and ability to overcome barriers and to achieve their goals. Your application will be evaluated on your (1) individual determination to succeed (2) future goals and plans to achieve them (3) ability to communicate the hardships you have overcome or currently face (4) self-motivation in completing challenging coursework (5) demonstrated need for financial assistance.

Amount:	(300) $20,000
Deadline:	January 15th
Contact:	apply@dellscholars.org
Telephone:	1-800-294-2039
Website:	http://www.dellscholars.org/

Don't Be Trashy Scholarships

Overview: Recycling Matters. Help pass it on. The average person throws out four pounds of trash per day. That's a lot of wasted opportunity. Empty bottles can become new bottles. Cans become more cans. You get the idea. Dosomething.org and Nestle waters North America are saying "Don't Be Trashy", recycle instead! Teens share stats on recycling and inspire their friends to take action. Every teen that shares a stat and completes a project is entered for a chance to win free movie tickets and college scholarships.

Eligibility Requirements: Applicants must sign up on the sponsor's website and start and complete a recycling project. The

Contest is only open and offered to legal residents of the 50 United States and the District of Columbia who, at the time of entry, are 18-25 years of age and are members in good standing of Do Something (membership is free and eligible persons may sign up at www.dosomething.org/user/register). Void in Puerto Rico and where prohibited. Employees, directors, officers, contractors and agents of the Sponsor, DoSomething.org, Campaign Partner, Nestle Waters North America and each of their respective parent entities, subsidiaries and affiliated companies, advertising, promotion and production agencies, web masters and we suppliers, and IRS dependents, immediate family members (parent, child, spouse and sibling) and individuals residing in their same household of each such employee, director, officer, contractor and agent are not eligible to participate. (See official scholarship rules)

Amount:	(10) $500 awards
Deadline:	April 22nd
Address:	Do Something, Inc.
	24-32 Union Square East, 4th Floor
	New York, NY 10003
Contact:	trashy@dosomething.org
Telephone:	(212) 254-2390
Website:	http://www.dosomething.org/trashy

Elks National Foundation
(Most Valuable Student Competition)

Overview: The Elks National Foundation will award 500 four-year scholarships to the highest-rated applicants in the competition.

Eligibility Requirements: Any high school senior who is a citizen of the United States is eligible to apply. Applicants must be citizens of the United States on the date their applications are signed; permanent legal resident status does not qualify. Male and female students compete separately. Applicants will be judged on scholarship, leadership, and financial need. All scholarships are in the form of certificates of award conditional upon the full-time enrollment of the winner in an accredited U.S. college or university. Applications must advance through local, district and state competitions to reach national judging. The Chicago office of the Elks National Foundation will notify the 500 national finalists by email in late February. To be eligible for an award, national finalists will be required to submit a secondary application online. The national finalists will also be required to mail their Student Aid Report to the Elks National Foundation. These applications are due March 25th. The Chicago office of the Elks National Foundation will announce the 500 national winners, and notify them in writing, by mid-April. (Many local Lodges, districts and state Elks associations award their own scholarships through this program. These scholarships are not to be confused with the 500 Elks National Foundation Most Valuable Student Scholarships.) Ranging from $1,000 per year to $15,000 per year, Most Valuable Student scholarships are for students pursuing a four-year degree, on a full-time basis (minimum of 12 semester hours), in a U.S. college or university. Applicants need not be related to a member of the Elks. College students are not eligible to apply.

Amount: (500) awards ranging from $1,000 per year to $15,000 per year

Deadline: December 2nd

Address: Elks National Foundation
2750 North Lakeview Avenue
Chicago, IL 60614-2256

Contact: enf@elks.org

Telephone: (773) 755-4728

Fax: (773) 755-4729

Website: http://www.elks.org/enf/scholars/mvs.cfm

Epic Book Drive

Overview: Donate your books to help low-income families in your community. By participating and sharing your book drive story, your team could win scholarship money! The book drive that collects the most books will win.

Eligibility Requirements: The Scholarship contest and Kindle Fire Sweepstakes (the "Promotion") is only open to legal residents of the 50 United States and District of Columbia and Canada who are younger than 26 years old as of the final date of entry, except officers, directors, members, and employees of the Sponsor, the judging organization (if applicable), or any other party associated with the development or administration of this Promotion, and the immediate family (i.e., parents, children, siblings, spouse), and persons residing in the same household, as such individuals. This Promotion is void outside the 50 United States and the District of Columbia and Canada, and where prohibited. Each participant entering the promotion for scholarships must report back to DoSomething.org at www.dosomething.org/epic under the "Tell Us About It" section with a detailed account of the book drive they organized in their community with photo verification. Reporting back may include, but is not limited to photos, videos, and written testimonials. (See official scholarship rules)

Amount:	$1,000 scholarship for an individual or $10,000 for their group (up to 10 members)
Deadline:	May 18th
Address:	Do Something, Inc.
	24-32 Union Square East, 4th Floor
	New York, NY 10003
Contact:	epic@dosomething.org.
Telephone:	(212) 254-2390
Website:	www.dosomething.org/epic

The Foot Locker Scholar Athletes Program

Overview: The Foot Locker Scholar Athletes program honors high school athletes for flexing their hearts on their sports team and in their communities. So, we're celebrating you - not just because you scored the winning touchdown or goal - but because you've used sports to become a strong leader and volunteer in your community.

Eligibility Requirements: Applicants must be currently involved in high school sports, intramural sports, or community based sports; have a minimum GPA of 3.0; be college bound (accredited four-year college) anticipated in Fall of the current academic year; be born on or after 9/1/1991; be a U.S. citizen or permanent legal resident (you will be asked to prove citizenship and age if you win). Officers, directors, members, and employees (including Store Associates) of Foot Locker Inc., Foot Locker Foundation Inc., or Do Something Inc. and any of their subsidiaries or divisions, are not eligible to apply, nor are members of the immediate family of anyone described above.

Amount:	(20) $20,000 awards
Deadline:	January 9th
Address:	Do Something, Inc.
	24-32 Union Square East, 4th Floor
	New York, NY 10003
Contact:	footlocker@dosomething.org.
Telephone:	(212) 254-2390
Website:	http://www.dosomething.org/footlocker

The Fountainhead Essay Contest

Overview: Ayn Rand's novels are inspiring and intellectually challenging. But they can also be financially rewarding for high school and college students. The Ayn Rand Institute sponsors annual essay contests that offer 680 prizes and over $99,000 in prize money every year.

Eligibility Requirements: No application is required. Contest is open to students worldwide. Entrant must write the essay and be in the 11th or 12th grade.

Amount:	First Prize: (1) $10,000 award, Second Prize: (5) $2,000 awards, Third Prizes: (10) $1,000 awards, Finalists: (45) $100 awards, Semi-finalists: (175) $50 awards
Deadline:	April 26th
Address:	The Fountainhead Essay Contest

The Ayn Rand Institute
P.O. Box 57044
Irvine, CA 92619-7044

Contact: info@aynrandnovels.com or essay@ aynrandnovels.com
Telephone: (949) 222-6550 ext. 247
Website: http://essaycontest.aynrandnovels.com/ TheFountainhead.aspx?theme=blue

---

The Gates Millennium Scholars Program

Overview: The Gates Millennium Scholars (GMS) Program, funded by a grant from the Bill & Melinda Gates Foundation, was established in 1999 to provide outstanding African American, American Indian/Alaska Native*, Asian Pacific Islander American**, and Hispanic American students with an opportunity to complete an undergraduate college education in any discipline area of interest. Continuing Gates Millennium Scholars may request funding for a graduate degree program in one of the following discipline areas: computer science, education, engineering, library science, mathematics, public health or science.

GMS will select 1,000 talented students each year to receive a good-through-graduation scholarship to use at any college or university of their choice. We provide Gates Millennium Scholars with personal and professional development through our leadership programs along with academic support throughout their college career.

Eligibility Requirements: Applicants must complete the following: 1. Student Application (Nominee Personal Information Form) 2. Educator's evaluation of the student's academic record (Nominator Form) 3. Evaluation of the student's community service and leadership activities (Recommender Form) by the deadline.

Amount: (1,000) Full collegiate expenses until graduation
Deadline: January 11th
Address: Gates Millennium Scholars

P.O. Box 1434
Alexandria, Virginia 22313
Telephone: 1-877-690-4677
Website: https://nominations.gmsp.org/GMSP%5FApp/

General Mills Federal Credit Union Scholarship

Overview: General Mills Federal Credit Union (GMFCU) is dedicated to furthering the financial education of our members and we are proud to be able to support members seeking higher education with the opportunity to apply for scholarships.

Eligibility Requirements: Applicants must be a member, or a joint owner of an account in good standing with GMFCU. Applicant must be planning to attend or already be enrolled in an undergraduate program at an accredited non-profit school, a public or private college, community college, or technical college (graduate schools do not qualify). Both traditional and non-traditional students are encouraged to apply. Scholarship recipients must begin studies at a qualified school within the current school year. Students must have a minimum GPA of 2.0. Recipients will be asked to provide proof of GPA in the form of a transcript. Recipients must be a U.S. citizen or a legal citizen of the U.S. All GMFCU Board Members, Supervisory Committee Members, staff, and the immediate family of those listed above are not eligible for consideration.

Amount: (1) $3,000 scholarship award (2) $2,000 scholarship awards (3) $1,000 scholarship awards
Deadline: January 31st
Contact: credit.union@gmfcu.com
Address: Scholarship Review Committee
General Mills Federal Credit Union
9999 Wayzata Blvd
Minnetonka, MN 55305
Telephone: 1-800-284-6328
Website: https://www.gmfcu.com/scholarship

Hispanic Scholarship Fund (General College Scholarship(s) Program)

Overview: The Hispanic Scholarship Fund (HSF) believes that the country prospers when all Americans have access to the opportunities a college education can afford. As the nation's leading Hispanic higher education fund, HSF works to address the barriers that keep many Latinos from earning a college degree. HSF/ General College Scholarships are designed to assist students of Hispanic heritage in obtaining a college degree. Scholarships are available on a competitive basis.

Eligibility Requirements: Applicants must be graduating High School Seniors, Community College Students, Community College Transfer Students, Undergraduate Students, or Graduate Students; of Hispanic heritage; a U.S. citizen or legal permanent resident with a permanent resident card or passport stamped I-551 (not expired); Have a minimum cumulative grade point average (GPA) of 3.0 on a 4.0 scale; Have plans to enroll full-time at a two or four year U.S. accredited institution in the U.S., Puerto Rico, U.S. Virgin Islands, or Guam during the current academic year; apply for federal financial aid by completing the *Free Application for Federal Student Aid (FAFSA)* and be pursuing his or her first undergraduate or graduate degree.

Amount:	$1,000 - $5,000
Deadline:	December 15th
Address:	Hispanic Scholarship Fund
	55 Second Street Suite 1500
	San Francisco, CA 94105
Contact:	scholar1@hsf.net or
	Saugustsson@hispanicfund.org
Telephone:	415-808-2300
Fax:	415-808-2301
Website:	http://www.hsf.net/innercontent.aspx?id=34

Horatio Alger National Scholarship Program

Overview: As one of the nation's largest college financial aid programs in the country, the Horatio Alger National Scholarship Program is the only major scholarship effort that specifically assists high school students who have faced and overcome great obstacles in their young lives. While many aid programs are directed primarily to recognizing academic achievement or leadership potential, the Horatio Alger program also seeks students who have a commitment to use their college degrees in service to others.

The National Scholarship Program is awarded to eligible students in all fifty states, the District of Columbia, and Puerto Rico. National Scholars receive an all expenses paid trip to Washington D.C. during the spring of their senior year to participate in the National Scholars Conference.

Eligibility Requirements: Applicants must be enrolled full time as a high school senior, progressing normally toward graduation, and planning to enter college no later than the fall following graduation; have a strong commitment to pursue and complete a bachelor's degree at an accredited institution located in the United States (students may start their studies at a two-year institution and then transfer to a four-year institution); critical financial need ($50,000 or less adjusted gross income per family is preferred; if higher, an explanation must be provided); involvement in co-curricular and community activities; demonstrate academic achievement (minimum grade point average of 2.0); and be a United States citizen.

Amount:	(104) $20,000 awards
Deadline:	Oct 30th, extended deadline Nov. 4th
Address:	Horatio Alger Scholarship Programs
	PO Box 4030
	Iowa City, IA 52243-4030
Contact:	HoratioAlger@act.org
Telephone:	(866) 763-9228
Website:	https://www.horatioalger.org/
	scholarships/program_national.cfm

Independence Day Essay Scholarship Contest

Overview: Write an essay on the assigned theme and develop the topic in any way you choose. Be creative! Essays will be evaluated based on the following criteria: Creativity, Theme Development, Clarity of Ideas, and Mechanics (Grammar, Spelling, Punctuation, Sentence Structure, etc.). Please review the Essay Rules

Eligibility Requirements: Applicants must be high school (9th—12th) students in a public, private, alternative, parochial school, or a home study program. Be U.S. citizens of all national backgrounds that are currently studying in the United States or in an American military school out of the country. *Be sure to download the rules and guidelines pdf*

Amount:	1st Place $5,000, 2nd Place (2) $500 awards, 3rd Place (1) $250
Deadline:	July 2nd
Address:	The Joe Foss Institute
	14415 N. 73rd St.
	Suite 109
	Scottsdale, AZ 85260
Contact:	Scholarship@JoeFoss.com
Telephone:	(480) 348-0316
Website:	http://www.joefoss.com

Jackie Robinson Foundation

Overview: The Jackie Robinson Foundation provides a multi-faceted experience designed to not only address the financial needs of minority students who aspire to attend college but also to guide them through the process of higher education, molding them into dynamic leaders with a commitment to public service and Jackie Robinson's humanitarian ideals. The award is given to outstanding high school graduates who plan to earn a baccalaureate degree from an accredited institution of higher education. Since its inception, the program has attracted the support of hundreds of companies, philanthropic institutions and individuals. As a result of our efforts, increasing numbers of students are able to attend the colleges and universities of their choice — where they are poised to develop their academic skills and leadership talents.

Eligibility Requirements: Applicant must be a graduating, minority high school senior; Plan to attend an accredited and approved four–year institution within the United States; Show leadership potential; Demonstrate a dedication to community service; Present evidence of financial need; Be a United States citizen; Have a minimum SAT score of 1,000 combined on the math and critical reading sections or a composite ACT score of 22; and Not possess a degree from a 2 or 4–year College when applying for the scholarship. The application package must include one (1) letter of recommendation and an official transcript (with raised seal). In addition, all applicants are required to take either the SAT or the ACT and submit their scores.

Amount:	$7,500 annually
Deadline:	March 30th
Contact:	scholarships@jackierobinson.org
Address:	Jackie Robinson Foundation
	One Hudson Square
	75 Varick Street 2nd Floor
	New York, NY 10013-1917
	Attn: Scholarship Application
Telephone:	(212) 290-8600
Fax:	(212) 290-8081
Website:	http://www.jackierobinson.org/apply /programs.php

John F. Kennedy Profile in Courage Essay Contest

Overview: The Profile in Courage Essay Contest invites United States high school students to consider the concept of political courage by writing an essay on a U.S. elected official who has chosen to do what is right, rather than what is expedient. A "Profile in Courage" essay is a carefully researched recounting of a story: the story of how an elected official risked his or her career to take a stand based on the dictates of conscience, rather than the dictates of polls, interest groups or even constituents. The contest challenges high school students to discover new profiles in courage, and to therefore research and write about acts of political courage that occurred after the publication of Kennedy's *Profiles in Courage* in 1956.

Eligibility Requirements: Applicants must be United States high school students in grades nine through twelve attending public, private, parochial, or home schools; U.S. students under the age of twenty enrolled in a high school correspondence/GED program in any of the fifty states, the District of Columbia, or the U.S. territories; and U.S. citizens attending schools overseas. Past winners and finalists are not eligible to participate. Employees of John Hancock Financial Services and members of their families are not eligible to participate.

Amount:	$10,000 ($5,000 cash award and $5,000 to grow in a John Hancock Freedom 529 College Savings Plan)
Deadline:	January 7th
Address:	John F. Kennedy Library Foundation Profile in Courage Essay Contest Columbia Point Boston, MA 02125
Contact:	foundation@jfklfoundation.org
Telephone:	(617) 514-1600
Website:	http://www.jfklibrary.org/Education/Profile-in-courage-essay-contest.aspx

Junior Achievement USA (Hugh B. Sweeny Achievement Award)

Overview: The Hugh B. Sweeny Achievement Award recognizes graduating seniors who demonstrate extraordinary results in impacting a community through entrepreneurship and similar initiatives.

Eligibility Requirements: Applicants must have completed

Junior Achievement Company Program or *JA Economics*; be a high school senior graduating before June 30; have minimum grade point average of 3.0; exemplify achievement, citizenship, creativity, leadership, motivation, and financial need; write a 500-word essay on the following topic: *Based on my experience and what I have learned in JA, what will it take to be a successful entrepreneur in tomorrow's economy? Why?*

Applicants will need: Recommendation Letters; Must provide three letters of recommendation supporting academic achievement, community involvement, and leadership skills.

Amount:	$5,000
Deadline:	February 1st
Address:	Junior Achievement Worldwide
	One Education Way
	Colorado Springs, Colorado 80906
Contact:	scholarships@ja.org
Telephone:	1-888-4-JA-ALUM
Fax:	(719) 540-6299
Website:	http://www.ja.org/programs/programs_ schol_hugh.shtml

KFC Colonel's Scholars Program

Overview: KFC Colonel's Scholars are looking for high school seniors with entrepreneurial drive, strong perseverance, demonstrated financial need and who want to pursue a college education at an accredited public institution in the state they reside. The KFC Colonel's Scholars Program is about you, your dreams and aspirations, and the perseverance to succeed. This program is offered to high school seniors planning to attend a public in-state college or university. Students who meet the criteria may apply online to become a KFC Colonel's Scholar.

Eligibility Requirements: Applicants must graduate from high school this academic year; Earn a minimum cumulative high school GPA of 2.75; Plan to pursue a bachelor's degree at a public, in-state college, or university; Be a US citizen or permanent resident; Demonstrate financial need. Scholars may begin their college career by entering into a 2-or 4-year accredited in-state college/university, as long as they stay on track to complete a bachelor's degree program.

Amount:	Up to $5,000 per year and up to $20,000 over four years
Deadline:	February 8th
Contact:	kfcscholars@act.org
Telephone:	1-866-532-7240
Website:	http://www.kfcscholars.org/

National Foster Parent Association, Inc.
(Gordon Evans Scholarship)

Overview: The National Foster Parent Association Scholarship Fund was established to benefit foster, adoptive and birth children of foster parent members. One scholarship each year is designated. The Gordon Evans Scholarship is in memory of a man who gave so much of himself to NFPA and the many children he fostered, as well as the untold numbers of people whose lives he affected. Five $1000 scholarships are awarded annually. Three scholarships are awarded to foster children, and two scholarships are awarded to birth or adoptive children of foster parent members. Each scholarship may be for college, vocational training or other educational pursuits. *Foster Parents must be members of NFPA.

Eligibility Requirements: Applicants must be in senior year of high school (regardless of age). Must provide a copy of high school transcript. Must provide documentation of cost from college/university. Must be accepted by an accredited college/university before receiving funding. (Include a copy of acceptance letter.) Include a minimum of two (2) letters of recommendation from: foster parent, social worker, residential center caregiver, teacher or guidance counselor, etc. with application. Include a typewritten statement of 300-500 words on, "Why I Want to Further My Education and Why I Should be considered for a National Foster Parent Association Scholarship."

Amount: (5) $1,000 awards
Deadline: March 31st
Address: National Foster Parent Association
                 2021 E Hennepin Ave #320
                 Minneapolis, MN 55413-1769
Contact: info@NFPAinc.org
Telephone: 1-800-557-5238
Fax: 1-888-925-5634
Website: http://www.nfpainc.org/

National Hook Up of Black Women, INC
(Arnita Y. Boswell Scholarship Award)

Overview: The Dr. Arnita Young Boswell Scholarship is awarded to African American freshman, sophomore, junior or senior students enrolled in an accredited college or university. The eligibility requirements are outlined in the current annual application.

Eligibility Requirements: Applicants must enter an accredited college or university as a freshman, sophomore, junior or senior. Have accumulative grade point average (GPA) of 2.75 or better from your previous or present institution. Be involved in school and community activities. Demonstrate a mastery of written communication skills in a 300 to 500-word essay. Complete application and return to the Scholarship Committee along with a 4x5 color photo or larger of yourself. Application must be accompanied by two current letters of recommendation (please ask writer to be specific) and written by a school and a community representative. Letters from supervisors and/or copies of certificates of participation from organizations where you performed your community service. (Applicant must have verified volunteer hours. Please be specific about your duties). Have the last school you attended submit an official transcript to the address below. An essay that adheres to the following standards must accompany application: Essay must contain 300 to 500 words or essay must be typed and double-spaced.

Amount: Minimum of (2) $500 rewards annually

Deadline: March 15th
Address: National Hook Up of Black Women Scholarship
Committee
3412 Blue Jay Drive
Tallahassee, FL 32305
Contact: Ms. Barbara R. Harvey, Chairperson
Telephone: (773) 667-7061
Fax: (773) 667-7064
Website: http://www.nhbwinc.com/contact.html

National Merit Scholarship Corporation
(National Achievement Scholarship Program)

Overview: The National Achievement® Scholarship Program is an academic competition established in 1964 to provide recognition for outstanding Black American high school students. Black students may enter both the National Achievement Program and the National Merit® Program by taking the Preliminary SAT/National Merit Scholarship Qualifying Test (PSAT/NMSQT®) and meeting other published requirements for participation. The two annual programs are conducted concurrently but operated and funded separately. A student's standing is determined independently in each program. Black American students can qualify for recognition and be honored as Scholars in both the National Merit Program and the National Achievement Program, but can receive only one monetary award from NMSC.

Eligibility Requirements: Applicants must Take the PSAT/NMSQT® in the specified year of the high school program and no later than the third year in grades 9 through 12, regardless of grade classification or educational pattern; Request entry to the National Achievement Program by marking Section 14 on the PSAT/NMSQT answer sheet, thereby identifying himself or herself as a Black American who wishes to be considered in this competition as well as in the National Merit® Scholarship Program; Be enrolled as a high school student, progressing normally toward graduation or completion of high school, and planning to enroll full time in college no later than the fall following completion of high school; and be a citizen of the United States; or be a U.S. lawful permanent resident (or have applied for permanent residence, the application for which has not been denied) and intend to become a U.S. citizen at the earliest opportunity allowed by law.

Amount: (700) $2500
Deadline: October 14th
Address: National Merit Scholarship Corporation
National Achievement Scholarship Program
1560 Sherman Avenue
Suite 200
Evanston, Illinois 60201-4897
Telephone: (847) 866-5100
Fax: (847) 866-5113
Website: http://nationalmerit.org/

National Merit Scholarship Program

Overview: The National Merit® Scholarship Program is an academic competition for recognition and scholarships that began in 1955. High school students enter the National Merit Program by taking the Preliminary SAT/National Merit Scholarship Qualifying Test (PSAT/NMSQT®) a test, which serves as an initial screen of more than 1.5 million entrants each year–and by meeting published program entry/participation requirements.

Eligibility Requirements: Applicants must take the PSAT/NMSQT® in the specified year of the high school program and no later than the third year in grades 9 through 12, *regardless of grade classification or educational pattern*; be enrolled as a high school student, progressing normally toward graduation or completion of high school, and planning to enroll full time in college no later than the fall following completion of high school; and be a citizen of the United States; or be a U.S. lawful permanent resident (or have applied for permanent residence, the application for which has not been denied) and intend to become a U.S. citizen at the earliest opportunity allowed by law.

Amount:	(700) $2500
Deadline:	October 12th
Address:	National Merit Scholarship Corporation
	National Merit Scholarship Program
	1560 Sherman Avenue
	Suite 200
	Evanston, Illinois 60201-4897
Telephone:	(847) 866-5100
Fax:	(847) 866-5113
Website:	http://nationalmerit.org/nmsp.php

National Peace Essay Contest for High School Students

Overview: The Academy for International Conflict Management and Peace building is the education and training arm of the United States Institute of Peace and runs the National Peace Essay Contest based on the belief that questions about peace, justice, freedom, and security are vital to civic education. Each year over 1,100 students submit entries to the essay contest while thousands more participate in related writing and other classroom exercises in high schools around the country.

First-place state winners receive scholarships and are invited to Washington for a five-day awards program. The Institute pays for expenses related to the program, including travel, lodging, meals and entertainment. This unique five-day program promotes an understanding of the nature and process of international peacemaking by focusing on a region and/ or them related to the current essay contest.

Eligibility Requirements: Students are eligible to participate if they are: In grades nine through twelve in any of the fifty states, the District of Colombia, the U.S. territories, or if they are U.S. citizens attending high school overseas. Students may be attending a public, private, or parochial school. Entries from home-schooled students are also accepted. Previous honorable mentions are eligible to enter. Previous first-place state winners and immediate relatives of directors or staff of the Institute are not eligible to participate. Students must choose a contest coordinator who can review the essays and act as the key contact between participants and the Institute. It is to the student's advantage to have a coordinator review the essay to make sure it is complete, has all the necessary forms, is free from typographical and grammatical errors, and addresses the topic. See the coordinator webpage for further information about the contest coordinator. *We encourage students of all backgrounds and ability to participate in the contest.*

Amount:	3 National Awards -1st place $10,000, 2nd place $5,000, 3rd place $2,500, 53 State Awards – 1st place $1,000
Deadline:	February 1st
Address:	United States Institute of Peace National Peace Essay Contest 2301 Constitution Avenue, NW Washington, DC 20037
Contact:	essaycontest@usip.org
Telephone:	(202) 429-1985
Fax:	(202) 429-6063
Website:	http://usip.org/npec

Optimist International Essay Contest

Overview: The Essay Contest is sponsored by Optimist International to give young people the opportunity to write about their own opinions regarding the world in which they live. The approach can encompass a young person's personal experience, the experience of their country or a more historical perspective. In additional to developing skills for written expression, participants also have the opportunity to win a college scholarship!

Eligibility Requirements: The Essay Contest is for students under 18 years of age as of December 31st of the current school year who have not yet graduated from high school or the equivalent and attend school in the United States, Canada or the Caribbean. Students residing on U.S. military bases overseas are eligible to enter using their last U.S. home of record. All Club contests are held by early February of the academic year. Club contest winners progress to the District level. Interested students must submit an essay on the pre-assigned topic to their local Optimist Club.

Amount: Plaque and $2,500
Deadline: The deadline for Clubs to submit their winning essay to the District Chair is February 28th. The deadline for Districts to submit their winner's information to Optimist International is April 15th
Address: Optimist International Foundation
4494 Lindell Blvd.
St. Louis, MO 63108
Contact: programs@optimist.org
Website: http://www.optimist.org/e/visitor/ scholarships.cfm

Optimist International Oratorical Contest

Overview: Each contest is entered through your local Optimist Club. This organization does not offer any application-based or need-based scholarships. Some individual Clubs do, but this information is not available at the International Office. All communication should be made with an Optimist Club Member in your area.

Eligibility Requirements: The Oratorical Contest is for students under 18 years of age as of December 31st of the current school year who have not yet graduated from high school or the equivalent and attend school in the United States, Canada or the Caribbean. Contest entry ends by late March of the academic year. Each applicant is required to give a 4- to 5-minute speech. Club contest winners progress to the District level. Interested students submit a speech on the pre-assigned topic to their local Optimist Club.

Amount: Plaque and $2,500
Deadline: *Students:* The deadline to enter is determined by the sponsoring Optimist Club. All Club-level contests are typically held by late March of the

current academic year. *Clubs and Districts:* The District deadline to submit winners to Optimist International is June 15, of the current academic year. Optimist International does not set Club/Zone/Regional deadlines.

Address: Optimist International Foundation
494 Lindell Blvd.
St. Louis, MO 63108

Contact: programs@optimist.org

Telephone: (314) 371-6000 1-800-500-8130

Fax: 1-800-500-8130

Website: http://www.optimist.org/e/visitor/
scholarships.cfm

Portuguese-American Scholarship Foundation

Overview: The primary mission of the Portuguese-American Scholarship Foundation (PASF) is to provide financial assistance, in the form of scholarships, to qualified New Jersey students of Portuguese ancestry, who wish to further their post-secondary school education and gain greater access to a better way of life. The PASF grants scholarships to those students who are interested in pursuing a Bachelor's degree.

Eligibility Requirements: Applicants must be New Jersey High School Seniors that are Portuguese-born or that have a parent or grandparent that is Portuguese-born (proof may be required). Applicants must be U.S. citizens, or U.S. permanent residents, (alien Registration Card may be required). In addition, applicants must have been continuous residents of the state of New Jersey for the 12-month period immediately preceding the receipt of the award. Applicant must demonstrate financial need. (Specific details are outlined in the application). Applicants must be New Jersey high school seniors applying to, or accepted in, a four-year college or university curriculum leading to a baccalaureate degree. Applicants must meet minimum PASF academic standards, including a grade point average of B or better.

Amount: $8,000

Deadline:	March 15th
Address:	Portuguese-American
	Scholarship Foundation
	ATTN: Director, Scholarship Review Board
	P.O. Box 3848
	Union, NJ 07083
Contact:	pasf@vivaportugal.com
Website:	http://www.americo.net/vivaportugal/
	nj/org/pasf/index.htm

Proton OnSite Scholarship Program

Overview: Proton OnSite seeks to fuel the next generation of scientific innovation by recognizing and rewarding high school seniors who demonstrate outstanding achievement, excellence and promise in the fields of science and technology, and who plan to pursue further education in these fields. The Scholarship program's mission is to enable outstanding, promising and financially needy high school seniors to pursue higher education in the fields of science and technology.

Eligibility Requirements: Applicants must be a High school senior currently enrolled in a U.S. high school, a U.S. citizen, the student must have a minimum GPA of 3.6/4.0 (weighted) in high school, completed Proton Onsite Scholarship application, declared major in science or technology related discipline (or statement of intent to pursue a major in this field)

Amount:	(10) awards up to $100,000 total for up to four years.
Deadline:	February 10th
Address:	Proton OnSite Scholarship Program
	10 Technology Drive,
	Wallingford, CT 06492
Contact:	scholarshipinfo@protononsite.com
Telephone:	(203) 678-2000
Website:	http://protonenergyscholarship.org/about.asp

Prudential Spirit of Community Awards

Overview: The Prudential Spirit of Community Awards program is the United States' largest youth recognition program based exclusively on volunteer community service. The program was created in 1995 by Prudential in partnership with the National Association of Secondary School Principals (NASSP) to honor middle level and high school students for outstanding service to others at the local, state, and national level.

The program's goals are to applaud young people who already are making a positive difference in their towns and neighborhoods, and to inspire others to think about how they might contribute to their communities. Over the past 16 years, more than 310, 000 young Americans have participated in the program, and nearly 100,000 of them have been officially recognized for their volunteer work.

Eligibility Requirements: Applicants must be in grades 5-12 as of November 1st, live in the 50 states or Washington, D.C., have conducted a volunteer service activity within 12 months prior to the date of application, and submit a completed application to a school principal or the head of an officially designated local organization by November 1st.

Amount: (102) $1,000 awards and an all expense paid trip to Washington D.C.

Deadline: November 1st

Address: International Scholarship and Tuition Services
200 Crutchfield Avenue
Nashville, TN 37210

Contact: info@applyists.com

Telephone: 1-877-525-8491, (615) 320-3149

Fax: (615) 627-9685

Website: http://spirit.prudential.com

Ron Brown Scholar Program

Overview: The Ron Brown Scholar Program seeks to identify African-American high school seniors who will make significant contributions to society.

Eligibility Requirements: Applicants must Excel academically, Exhibit exceptional leadership potential, Participate in community service activities & demonstrate financial need. The applicant must be a US citizen or hold a permanent resident visa card. Current college students are not eligible to apply.

Amount:	(10-20) $10,000 awards annually up to $40,000 for four years
Deadline:	November 1st - application will be considered for the Ron Brown Scholar Program AND forwarded to a select and limited number of additional scholarship providers. January 9th - final application must be postmarked deadline in order to be considered for only the Ron Brown Scholar Program only.
Address:	Ron Brown Scholar Program 1160 Pepsi Place, Suite 206 Charlottesville, VA 22901
Contact:	info@ronbrown.org
Telephone:	(434) 964-1588
Fax:	(434) 964-1589
Website:	http://www.ronbrown.org/Home.aspx

Rosa L. Parks Scholarship

Overview: The Rosa L. Parks Scholarship Foundation is dedicated to awarding scholarships to Michigan high school seniors who hold close to Mrs. Parks' ideals while demonstrating academic skills, community involvement and economic need.

Eligibility Requirements: Applicants must be a senior attending a public or private Michigan High School; Graduate by August of the application year; Have GPA of 2.5 or above; complete an application form and essay; Furnish official copies of high school transcript and ACT or SAT results and, meet additional requirements as noted in application package.

Amount:	(40) $2,000
Deadline:	August 24th
Address:	The Rosa L. Parks Scholarship Foundation
	P.O. Box 950
	Detroit, MI 48231
Contact:	rpscholarship@dnps.com
Telephone:	(313) 222-2538
Website:	http://www.rosaparksscholarshipfoundation.org

SALEF's "Fulfilling Our Dreams Scholarship" Fund
(High school Student Scholarship)

Overview: SALEF's "Fulfilling Our Dreams Scholarship" fund is making higher education a reality for Central American and Latino students, including AB 540 students, with approximately 750 scholarships provided since 1998. SALEF's "Fulfilling Our Dreams Scholarship" Fund offers financial assistance and support to undergraduate, graduate and professional students, often making the difference in whether a student can attend college or not.

The Scholarships are open to all qualifying students regardless of immigration status. SALEF promotes giving back to our communities, thus scholarship recipients are expected to complete community service hours and receipt of the scholarship award is dependent on completion of their pledge.

Eligibility Requirements: Applicants must be of Central American or other Latino ethnicity. Applicants must demonstrate proven financial need. Applicants must possess a minimum 2.5 GPA. Applicants must demonstrate a history of community involvement. Applicants must be either:

a) Graduating High School seniors
b) Current undergraduate, graduate, and professional students
c) Community college students (must be AB540)

d) Vocational/Trade school (must be pursuing a health related field)

We prioritize in low-income students that reside and study in either one of the following areas:

a) Greater Los Angeles Area Specifically South Central Los Angeles, Pico Union-Central LA,
b) San Fernando Valley
c) San Francisco/Bay Area

Amount:	$1,000 - $5,000 renewable
Deadline:	May 2nd
Address:	Carlota Merino
	Scholarship Fund Coordinator
	1625 W. Olympic Blvd. Suite 718
	Los Angeles, CA 90015
Contact:	cmerino@salef.org
Telephone:	(213) 480-1052
Fax:	(213) 487-2530
Website:	http://salef.org

Siemens Merit Scholarship

Overview: The Siemens Merit Scholarship is an independent, not for profit organization. Their purpose is to provide a system to identify and honor exceptional high school students for corporations, foundations and other organizations that wish to sponsor college undergraduate scholarships.

Eligibility Requirements: Applicants must be employees whose children are currently in their junior year. Siemens Merit Scholarships will be awarded in the spring of the student's senior year. Children of employees who will complete high school and enroll full time in college in the following year must take the PSAT/NMSQT in the fall of the current academic year, on the date their school chooses for the administration. At the beginning of the school year, the student should obtain a copy of the current Official Student Guide to the PSAT/NMSQT from the high school counselor and make arrangements with the school to take the PSAT/NMSQT in October. Each student (or parent on behalf of the student) is required to submit a completed Siemens Merit Scholarship Program Entry Form by April 1st. Eligible divisions: Siemens Building Technologies, Siemens Corporation, Siemens Energy, Siemens Energy & Automation, Siemens Financial Services, Siemens Hearing Instruments, Siemens Medical Solutions USA, Siemens Product Lifecycle Management, Siemens Transportation Systems, Siemens Water Technologies.

Amount: $4,000 ($1,000 per year)
Deadline: April 1st
Address: Siemens Foundation
170 Wood Avenue South
Iselin, NJ 08830
Contact: Kiesha.Boykins@siemens.com ,
Foundation.us@siemens.com
Telephone: 1-877-822-5233
Fax: (732) 603-5890
Website: http://www.siemens-foundation.org/en/
merit_scholarship.htm

The Sons of Portugal Scholarship

Overview: The Sons of Portugal Scholarship was established in 1965 with the primary objective of recognizing and rewarding academic excellence among students of Portuguese descent.

Eligibility Requirements: Applicant must be of Portuguese descent living at least one full year in Danbury or its surrounding areas. Applicant or his/her parent(s) must be an active member of at least one of the following organizations and/or its active groups: Portuguese Cultural Center or Immaculate Heart of Mary Parish, Danbury. Scholarships will be granted to any accredited educational institution up to a maximum of four years per recipient.

Amount: 1st place $3,000, 2nd place $2,500, 3rd place $2,000, 4th place $1,500, 5th place $1,000 (All

	awards are renewable up to four years.)
Deadline:	April 7th
Address:	Danny Martins
	℅ The Sons of Portugal Scholarship Committee
	8 Wilkes Rd.
	Danbury, CT 06811
Telephone:	(203) 748-1278
Website:	http://www.portugueseculturalcenter.com/
	organizations/scholarship

Step Up to Bullying Scholarship

Overview: In the U.S., 160,000 kids stay home every day to avoid being bullied. DoSomething.org is teaming up with a new nationally-released documentary, BULLY, to help teens everywhere tell the world what's really going on in their schools. Take the DoSomething.org Bully Project quiz to tell us how bullying goes down in your school. Want another reason to participate? If you complete the quiz, you'll be entered to win scholarships! If you share the quiz with your friends, and thus spread the movement to end bullying, the amount of scholarships will increase up to $20,000.

Eligibility Requirements: This contest (the "Promotion") is only open to citizens and legal residents of the United States, who are between 13 and 25 years of age as of the contest entry date. Officers, directors, members, and employees of the Sponsor; the judging organization (if applicable); or any other party associated with the development or administration of this Promotion, and the immediate family (i.e., parents, children, siblings, spouse), and persons residing in the same household, of such individuals are excluded from winning the contest. This Promotion is void outside of the United States, and where prohibited. All entries become the property of the Sponsor and will not be acknowledged or returned. Limit: One entry per person and per e-mail address during the Promotion Period. All entrant information, including e-mail addresses, is subject to the respective Privacy Policy of the applicable Sponsor.

Amount:	Up to $20,000
Deadline:	May 9th
Address:	Do Something, Inc.
	24-32 Union Square East, 4th Floor
	New York, NY 10003
Contact:	bully@dosomething.org
Telephone:	(212) 254-2390
Website:	http://www.dosomething.org/bully

Stuck at Prom Scholarship

Overview: The Stuck at Prom® Scholarship Contest challenges students to create and accessorize their prom outfits with duct tape, then wear them to prom for a chance to win scholarship cash prizes.

Eligibility Requirements: The Contest is open to legal residents of the United States and Canada, including the District of Columbia, but excluding Colorado, Maryland, Vermont, Puerto Rico and the Province of Quebec, 14 years of age or older at the time of entry who are attending a high school, home school association or other school-sanctioned prom in 2012, and who submit their Contest Entry by the deadline. Employees of Sponsor, their family members, and persons living in the same household as employees or their family members are NOT eligible. All federal, state and local laws apply.

Contest participants must enter as a couple (two individuals) ("Entrant" or "Entrant Couple"). Each couple must attend a high school, home school association or other school-sanctioned prom held in 2012, wearing complete prom attire and/or accessories made using Duck® brand duct tape ("Duct Tape Prom Attire"), and submit their Contest Entry by the contest deadline. Other materials, in addition to duct tape, may be used or incorporated into the design. The prom attire must be an original creation made by the couple, and may not copy, incorporate or be based on the work of a third party – any entry as such is subject to disqualification at the discretion of Sponsor (see section entitled "No Infringement"). Contest Entries must be submitted online by going to www.stuckatprom.com

Amount:	1st place $5,000 2nd place $3,000 3rd place $2,000 7 runner-ups $500 each
Deadline:	June 12th
Address:	ShurTech Brands
	Attn: Consumer Relations
	32150 Just Imagine Dr.
	Avon, OH 44011
Telephone:	1-800-321-1733
Website:	www.stuckatprom.com

Tall Clubs International

Overview: Annually, at TCI Convention, TCI awards student scholarship(s) of up to $1000 each to tall students who are under 21 years of age and attending their first year of college in the following fall. TCI has forms that are downloadable by any Club member in the member services console pertaining to student scholarship candidate submissions by Clubs to the TCI Foundation Scholarship Committee prior to a cut off deadline date. The TCI Foundation then determines from these submitted candidates, who the scholarship award winner(s) are. The winner(s) are announced to the Clubs involved so they may make the scholarship presentations.

Eligibility Requirements: The recipients must also meet the TCI height requirement minimums of 5'10" for women and 6'2" for men. Contact a TCI Member Club closest to you for sponsorship. Even if they do not have an active Student Scholarship campaign, they may simply appoint you as their candidate. Select the TCI Member Club closest to you from the list of Member Clubs here at this website. This link will take you to a map. Click your state and see what TCI Clubs may be closest to you. If there is no club in your state, choose the one closest to you. Once you locate a TCI Member Club closest to you, send them an email to the listed address asking about their Student Scholarship program.

Amount:	$1,000

Deadline: See local chapter
Address: Tall Clubs International
8466 N. Lockwood Ridge Road 188
Sarasota, FL 34243
Contact: admin@tall.org
Telephone: 1-888-468-2552
Website: http://tall.org

Positive Coaching Alliance (PCA)
Triple-Impact Competitor Scholarships

Overview: PCA awards post-secondary education scholarships to dozens of high school athletes in selected geographic regions: Chicago, Houston, New York City Tri-State Area, Northern California and Washington, D.C.

Eligibility Requirements: Applications are based on essays by students explaining how their actions represent the ideal of the Triple-Impact Competitor®, who impacts sport on three levels by working to improve oneself, teammates and the game as a whole. There are awards ceremonies in various cities each autumn, which typically feature a local celebrity coach, athlete, team executive, or journalist.

Amount: $1,000-$3,000
Deadline: May 31st
Address: Positive Coaching Alliance
Triple-Impact Scholarship
1001 N. Rengstorff Ave. Suite 100
Mountain View, CA 94043
Contact: Courtney_pollack@positivecoach.org
Telephone: 1-866-725-0024
Website: http://www.positivecoach.org/our-programs/
triple-impact-competitor-scholarships/

Video Scholarship Contest

Overview: Create a video, no more than three minutes in length that inspires viewers and reminds them of why our freedoms, our

Constitution, and/or our Bill of Rights are worth defending. Tell a story. Interview a hero. Remind us what our freedoms cost. Help others learn why our founding documents matter to all Americans—or matter to you personally. Share how our freedoms have enabled or motivated you to make a difference. Alternatively, do something very different (while still following these themes, of course). Be creative! We want to be inspired, and we want your video to inspire others.

Eligibility Requirements: The Contest is open only to the following entrants: (i) all individuals, fourteen (14) years of age or older at the time of entry, (ii) who are currently enrolled in, or graduated within the previous twelve (12) months from, any public, private, alternative, parochial, or home-study high school-level educational program or institution designed to conclude with the awarding of a degree or diploma, and (iii) who are U.S. citizens or the legal residents of, and physically located within, any of the fifty (50) United States and the District of Columbia. Previous scholarship recipients of Sponsor are not eligible. Void where restricted or prohibited by law. All trustees, directors, officers, and employees of the Sponsor, Administrator, and of each of Sponsor's and Administrator's respective parent companies, subsidiaries, affiliates, sales representatives, distributors, licensees, agents, website administrators, advertising and Contest agencies, and any immediate family members (spouses, parents, children, and siblings and their respective spouses, regardless of where they reside) and those living in the same household (whether related or not) of any of the foregoing, are not eligible to participate in the Contest. *Be sure to download the rules and guidelines pdf.*

Amount:	1st place $10,000, 2nd place $1,000, 3rd place $500
Deadline:	October 23rd
Address:	The Joe Foss Institute
	14415 N. 73rd St.
	Suite 109
	Scottsdale, AZ 85260
Contact:	Scholarship@JoeFoss.com
Telephone:	(480) 348-0316

<u>**Website:**</u>   http://contest.joefoss.com

Veterans Day Essay Contest

Overview: Here is the challenge: Find a military veteran you don't already know. Get involved in that person's life. This is not simply an interview. Make a friend; discover his (or her) history, his feelings—then and now—and how he would like to spend the rest of his life. Write a 1500 word essay about the experience (and continue to cultivate the relationship, of course). Beyond the contest itself, our hope is that you will really enjoy the process of befriending a veteran.

<u>**Eligibility Requirements**</u>: The Contest is open only to the following entrants: (i) all individuals, fourteen (14) years of age or older at the time of entry, (ii) who are currently enrolled in, or graduated within the previous twelve (12) months from, any public, private, alternative, parochial, or home-study high school-level educational program or institution designed to conclude with the awarding of a degree or diploma, and (iii) who are U.S. citizens or the legal residents of, and physically located within, any of the fifty (50) United States and the District of Columbia. Previous scholarship recipients of Sponsor are not eligible. Void where restricted or prohibited by law. All trustees, directors, officers, and employees of the Sponsor, Administrator, and of each of Sponsor's and Administrator's respective parent companies, subsidiaries, affiliates, sales representatives, distributors, licensees, agents, website administrators, advertising and Contest agencies, and any immediate family members (spouses, parents, children, and siblings and their respective spouses, regardless of where they reside) and those living in the same household (whether related or not) of any of the foregoing, are not eligible to participate in the Contest. *See the rules and guidelines pdf.*

<u>**Amount:**</u>	1st place $5,000, 2nd place (2) $500 awards, 3rd place (1) $250
<u>**Deadline:**</u>	October 9th
<u>**Address:**</u>	The Joe Foss Institute

14415 N. 73rd St., Suite 109
Scottsdale, AZ 85260
Contact: Scholarship@JoeFoss.com
Telephone: (480) 348-0316
Website: http://www.joefoss.com,
http://www.joefoss.com/programs/scholarship-program/current-scholarship-essay-contest/127

Walmart Foundation Associate Scholarship

Overview: The Walmart Associate Scholarship is a college scholarship that is available to associates in any division of Walmart and Sam's Club. Associates must be based in the U.S. and should demonstrate financial need and involvement in their community.

The Walmart Associate Scholarship is available for associates seeking certificates, associates, bachelors, and graduate degrees through accredited institutions of higher education and for associates participating in the Lifelong Learning Program through American Public University. The Foundation accepts applications and awards Walmart Associate Scholarships four times a year.

Eligibility Requirements: Applicants must be a U.S. Citizen or Permanent Legal Resident of the United States, be employed part-time or full-time with any division of Walmart for at least six consecutive months prior to the appropriate application due date (see chart below), have graduated high school/home school or obtained a GED before applying or be a graduating high school senior. If applying as a graduating high school senior, Applicants must wait to apply until they are within 6 months of starting your college courses. Must have financial need and be able to demonstrate the need with required documents. (Note: Students with other funds that pay entirely for tuition, books, fees, and on-campus room and board are ineligible.)

Amount: Up to a maximum award of $16,000 over six years or to the attainment of the degree for which the scholarship was awarded, whichever occurs

first.
Deadline: September 1st, December 1st, March 1st, June 1st
Address: Walton Family Scholarship Program
PO Box 4030
Iowa City, IA 52243
Telephone: (479) 464-1570
Website: http://www.walmartstores.com/communitygiving

The Wal-Mart Dependent Scholarship

Overview: The Walmart Dependent Scholarship is a $13,000 scholarship paid out over four years. *Applicants must be dependents of Walmart or Sam's Club associates in any U.S. division, have at least a 2.0 high school GPA and prove financial need.

Eligibility Requirements: Applicants must be a U.S. Citizen or Permanent Legal Resident of the United States. Must be the dependent of an associate (employee) of any division of Wal-Mart who has been actively employed with Wal-Mart for at least six consecutive months as of March 15th of the current year. Dependents of Wal-Mart Board of Directors and dependents of Wal-Mart officers (vice president and above) are not eligible to apply. Must be a high school or home school senior graduating or earning a GED between August 1st and July 31st. Must have financial need and be able to demonstrate the need with required documents. (Note: Students with other funds that pay entirely for tuition, books, fees, and on-campus room and board are ineligible.)

Amount: $13,000
Deadline: March 15th
Address: Walton Family Scholarship Program
PO Box 4030
Iowa City, IA 52243
Telephone: (479) 464-1570
Website: http://www.walmartstores.com/communitygiving

Wells Fargo Educational Financial Services
(College Steps Scholarship Sweepstakes)

Overview: Wells Fargo offers two educational resource programs: one, for high school students called "CollegeSTEPS" and one for college students called "Student Education Resources" (collectively referred to as "Resources"). There is one enrollment form for both resources. You will be automatically assigned to the appropriate resource based on the information you provide on the enrollment form. Upon completing and submitting the enrollment form during the Promotion Period, you will be automatically entered in the Sweepstakes. To sign up for the resources go to wellsfargo.com/collegesteps and fully complete the "Enrollment Form." You will automatically receive one Sweepstakes entry when you enroll.

Eligibility Requirements: Applicants must enroll in Wells Fargo's CollegeSTEPS Program online.

Amount:	(20) $1,000 awards
Deadline:	August 5th
Address:	Wells Fargo Education Financial Services
	P.O. Box 5185
	Sioux Falls, SD 57117-5185
Fax:	1-800-456-0561
Website:	https://www.wellsfargo.com/collegesteps

Western Golf Association Evans Scholars Foundation
(Chick Evan Caddie Scholarships)

Overview: The Chick Evans Caddie Scholarship is a full tuition and housing college scholarship for golf caddies that is renewable for up to four years. Each year, more than 800 deserving caddies across the country attend college on a four-year scholarship from the Evans Scholars Foundation. Selected applicants must have a strong caddie record, excellent grades, outstanding character and demonstrated financial need.

Eligibility Requirements: To qualify, caddies must be

nominated by their club and meet four requirements:

Strong caddie record: Applicants must have caddied, successfully and regularly, for a minimum of two years and expected to caddie and/or work at their sponsoring club during the summer when they apply for the scholarship.

Excellent academics: Applicants must have completed their junior year of high school with above a B average in college preparatory courses and are required to take the ACT.

Demonstrated financial need: Applicants must clearly establish their need for financial assistance.

Outstanding character: Applicants must be outstanding in character, integrity, and leadership. Applicants are evaluated and compete on the above criteria for the limited number of Chick Evans Caddie Scholarships awarded annually. The Scholarship Committee will interview finalists and the final selection rests with the Committee. Almost all Evans Scholars attend one of the 14 universities where the Foundation maintains a Scholarship House. An Evans Scholar is asked to fulfill four requirements: Maintain a strong academic record, be actively involved in house and campus affairs, respect their fellow scholar, and faithfully perform assigned house duties.

Amount:	(800) Full-Tuition
Deadline:	August 1st
Address:	Western Golf Association
	One Briar Road
	Golf, IL 60029
Telephone:	(847) 724-4600
Fax:	(847) 724-7133
Website:	http://www.wgaesf.org

The United States Senate Youth Program)

Overview: The United States Senate Youth Program (USSYP) is an intensive week-long educational experience and scholarship sponsored by the United States Senate for outstanding high school students who are interested in pursuing careers in public service. If you are a high school junior or senior already serving as an elected official in your student body or other state or community organization, you may already be qualified to apply.

Eligibility Requirements: Applicants must be any high school junior or senior student is eligible for the program provided he or she has not previously been a delegate to Washington Week and has not received a USSYP scholarship. The student is required to be currently serving in an elected or appointed capacity in any one of the following student government, civic or educational organizations:

a.   Student Body President, Vice President, Secretary or Treasurer
b.   Class President, Vice President, Secretary or Treasurer
c.   Student Council Representative
d.   Student representative elected or appointed (appointed by a panel, commission or board) to a district, regional or state-level civic and/or educational organization approved by the state selection administrator.

Each student must be a PERMANENT RESIDENT of the United States and currently enrolled in a public or private secondary school located in the state (including for these purposes the District of Columbia) in which either one of his or her parents or guardians legally resides. A student attending a school which is located in a state other than the state of legal residence of either one of such student's parents or guardians is not eligible.
Exceptions to the permanent residency requirement will only be made in the following cases:

a.   Students from the Department of Defense Education Activity will represent the state(s) of which the parents/guardians are U.S. legal voting residents.
b.   Interstate Compacts (by Congressional mandate) presently exist between New Hampshire-Maine and New Hampshire-Vermont, authorizing school districts to

legally cross state borders. Students in these schools are eligible to make an application for this program only through the states where the schools are located.

Amount:	(104) $5,000
Deadline:	See each state deadline on website
Address:	The United States Senate Youth Program
	90 New Montgomery St. Suite 1212
	San Francisco, CA 94105-4504
Contact:	Rayne Guilford, Director, Lynn DeSmet,
	Deputy Director
Telephone:	(415) 908-4540
Fax:	(415) 348-0887
Website:	www.ussenateyouth.org

Vegetarian Resource Group Scholarship

Overview: Due to the generosity of an anonymous donor, The Vegetarian Resource Group each year will award $10,000 in college scholarship money to graduating U.S. high school students who have promoted vegetarianism in their schools and/or communities. Vegetarians do not eat meat, fish, or fowl. Applications can be postmarked by the deadline date and early submission is encouraged.

Eligibility Requirements: Applicants will be judged on having shown compassion, courage, and a strong commitment to promoting a peaceful world through a vegetarian diet/lifestyle. Payment will be made to the student's college (U.S. based only). Winners of the scholarships give permission to release their names to the media. Applications and essays become property of The Vegetarian Resource Group. We may ask finalists for more information. Scholarship winners are contacted by telephone.

Amount:	(2) $5,000 awards
Deadline:	February 20th
Address:	The Vegetarian Resource Group
	P.O. Box 1463,
	Baltimore, MD 21203

Contact:	vrg@vrg.org
Telephone:	(410) 366-8343
Website:	http://www.vrg.org/student/scholar.htm

Young Naturalist Scholarship

Overview: The Young Naturalist Awards is a research-based science competition for students in grades 7-12 to promote participation and communication in science. Participants are expected to conduct their investigations with honesty and integrity. The presentation of another's work as your own, plagiarism, or the fabrication or use of false data will disqualify a student from this and future Young Naturalist Awards competitions.

Eligibility Requirements: Applicants must be a student in grades seven through twelve and are currently enrolled in a public, private, parochial, or home school in the United States, Canada, the U.S. territories, or if you are a citizen in a U.S.-sponsored school abroad, you are eligible to enter. Applicants that are: Sons and daughters of American Museum of Natural History employees or consultants are not eligible to enter the Young Naturalist Awards.

Amount:	Twelve cash awards, two for each grade level, will be awarded to the authors of the winning essays. Cash awards are as follows: (2) 7th grade: $500, (2) 8th grade: $750, (2) 9th grade: $1,000, (2) 10th grade: $1,500, (2) 11th grade: $2,000, (2) 12th grade: $2,500
Deadline:	March 9th
Address:	Young Naturalist Awards Administrator National Center for Science Literacy, Education, and Technology American Museum of Natural History Central Park West at 79th St New York, NY, 10024
Telephone:	(212) 769-5606
Fax:	(212) 769-5427

Website: http://www.amnh.org/nationalcenter/
youngnaturalistawards/read.html

Youth For Understanding (YFU) USA (Study Abroad Scholarship)

Overview: Through the generosity of numerous corporations, governments, foundations, and individuals, you have the chance to win a full or partial scholarship to live overseas as a YFU exchange student.

Eligibility Requirements: YFU looks for students who are flexible, have a spirit of adventure, and who will enjoy the challenge of adapting to new people in a new culture. Please be sure to review the information on the individual scholarship information sheets carefully before completing your application. Generally, the following information applies to most programs.

Program Dates: Year, semester, and summer scholarship dates correspond to YFU program dates. See individual country pages for more information. Here is a general outline of dates:

- Year programs begin in July, August, or September and end in June or July of the following year (summer departure) or begin in January and end in December or January (winter departure). Programs to Japan depart in March.
- Semester programs begin in July, August, or September and end in December of the same year or January of the following year, except for programs to Japan, which begin in March and end in the summer.
- Summer programs begin in June or July and end in late July or early August of the same year.

Country Selection: Many scholarships are designated for a specific country. Others allow you to list several country choices. You should think carefully about which countries interest you most. YFU will make every effort to assign you to one of your top country choices, but reserves the right to place you in any country specified by the scholarship program for which you are applying. Please review the individual scholarship information sheets to determine the specific country options available for your scholarship program.

Academic Requirements: For most year and semester programs, a "B" average or better (3.0 on a 4.0 scale) is required. For summer programs, a "C" average or better (2.0 on a 4.0 scale) is required; however, a 3.0 GPA or higher may be required in some cases.

Language Requirements: Most countries do not require previous language study. As a few countries do require previous language study, please consult the individual country pages for eligibility requirements by selecting from the Countries drop-down menu on the left of the website.

Age and Health Requirements: You must be between 15 and 18 years old and in good physical and emotional health.

Amount:	Varies according to program of study
Deadline:	Year programs begin in July, August, or September and end in June or July of the following year (summer departure) or begin in January and end in December or January (winter departure**)**. Programs to Japan depart in March.
	Semester programs begin in July, August, or September and end in December of the same year or January of the following year, except for programs to Japan, which begin in March and end in the summer.
	Summer programs begin in June or July and end in late July or early August of the same year.
Address:	Youth For Understanding USA
	6400 Goldsboro Road Suite 100
	Bethesda, MD 20817
	United States of America
Telephone:	(240) 235-2100
Website:	http://yfuusa.org/american-students.php

Your Point of View" Contest

Overview: Energize Students asked teenagers ages 14 - 19 years old, "What would you like to change about your education?" and "How would you change it?" We wanted to know what would make high school more valuable to students and give them the opportunity to be part of the solution. We understand that students see the issues and have ideas to fix them, so we gave students a forum to be heard by submitting essays

Eligibility Requirements: To enter, you must submit an essay that illustrates changes that you believe your high school needs. The top ideas and stories will be asked to be part of a feature length documentary and the top three submissions will also receive funds towards their education.

Employees of EnergizeStudents.org, its respective parent, affiliates, subsidiaries, advertising sponsors and promotional agencies, and the immediate family members of each are not eligible.

Amount:	1st place $1,000, 2nd place $500, 3rd place $300
Deadline:	November 1st
Address:	Energize Students
	New Hope Charitable Foundation
	125 Linda Vista Dr., Suite 101
	San Marcos, CA 92078-3819
Contact:	Contest@EnergizeStudents.org
Telephone:	(760) 591-0719
Website:	http://www.energizestudents.org/Speak-Your-Mind/Contest.aspx

Youth Foundation Hadden Scholarship

Overview: Youth Foundation's basic objective is the awarding of Hadden Scholarships to exceptionally worthy, financially needy, Secondary school seniors for their undergraduate college education. The Scholarship Committee selects the recipients after carefully evaluating character, scholastic records, financial need, extra-curricular activities, and employment experience. No scholarship is given to a student unless his or her college has agreed to refrain from reducing its own scholarship grant at the expense of the Youth Foundation's award. Youth Foundation encourages young people to establish permanent attitudes of self-reliance, confidence, self-discipline, responsibility, volunteerism, and exemplary character thereby benefiting their own lives, and more importantly, the lives of others.

Eligibility Requirements: Applicants must be graduating high school seniors, who are United States citizens, seeking higher education at accredited four-year United States colleges or universities. Applicants must show a 3.5+ or better grade point average and should document financial need.

In addition, the Foundation strongly encourages extra-curricular and community activities on the part of its applicants demonstrating a strong desire to help others.

Amount:	Grants have ranged from $2,500 to $4,000 per year and are renewable for a total of four years of undergraduate scholarship funding at our discretion. Individual scholarship size may fluctuate over time depending upon the size of our endowment
Deadline:	March 15th
Address:	Youth Foundation
	317 Madison Avenue, Suite 824
	New York, NY 10017
Telephone:	(212) 840-6291
Website:	http://foundationcenter.org/ grantmaker/youthfdn/about.html

COLLEGE SCHOLARSHIPS

* While the author has done his best to make sure all information in this section is accurate and up to date, all scholarship deadlines are subject to change at the sponsor's discretion. You should double-check all deadlines on each scholarships website for the most up to date information.
() Parenthesis indicate the quantity of scholarships available

American Association of Japanese Women

Overview: AAJUW seeks to promote the education of women, as well as to contribute to U.S. – Japan relations, cultural exchanges, and development of leadership.

Eligibility Requirements: Applicants must be a female student enrolled in an accredited California college or university. Have junior, senior, or graduate standing by the fall of the upcoming year. Attend, at your own expense, the award ceremony held in January of each year. Demonstrate a desire and intent to fulfill a leadership role in your chosen field of study and to be a contributor to improved U.S.-Japan relations and cultural exchanges. Must not have received an AAJUW scholarship before.

Amount: $2,000
Deadline: October 31st
Address: AAJUW Scholarship Committee
3543 West Blvd.
Los Angeles, CA 90016
Contact: Dr. Akiko Agishi, scholarship@aajuw.org
Website: www.aajuw.org/Scholarship.htm

American Cancer Society College Scholarship Program (R.O.C.K)

Overview: The American Cancer Society's R.O.C.K. College Scholarship Program is an award-winning college scholarship opportunity exclusively for students with a history of cancer. The program gives young cancer survivors a chance to pursue an undergraduate degree from an accredited Florida university, community college, or vocational technical school.

Eligibility Requirements: Applicants must be Florida residents, Personal diagnosis of cancer before age 21, Under 21 at the time of application, attend an accredited college, university or vocational school in Florida during the academic year

Amount:	$3,000 total - 2,700 towards tuition, $300 towards textbooks
Deadline:	April 10th
Address:	Director of Childhood Cancer Programs American Cancer Society 3709 West Jetton Avenue City, Tampa, FL 33629
Contact:	susan.lee@cancer.org
Telephone:	1-800-444-1410, ext. 4405
Website:	http://www.cancer.org/inyourarea/ florida/programsandservices/rockscholarship

American Federation of Teachers (AFT)
Robert G. Porter Scholars Program

Overview: With input from AFT leaders, members and staff, and with the wholehearted approval and direction of the Porter family, the Robert G. Porter Scholars Program was established through a resolution passed by the AFT executive council in 1992. There could be no finer way "to recognize the contributions and memory of Robert G. Porter, in perpetuity" than to foster the education of AFT members and their families, reasoned the drafters of the resolution. A mix of national AFT contributions and voluntary contributions from AFT affiliates, members and friends make the scholars program possible for two purposes: to encourage members in good standing to learn more about labor or further their own career, and to support members' dependents.

Eligibility Requirements:

(10) One-time $1,000 Grant

- Must be an AFT member in good standing for at least one year.
- Pursuing courses in their field of work.
- No full or part-time AFT staff, state or local, may apply.

<u>Four-year $8,000 Postsecondary Scholarship</u>

- Must be an AFT member's dependent.
- Graduating high school senior.
- Parent or guardian must be an AFT member for at least one year.

Amount: (1) $8,000 (10) $1,000
Deadline: March 31st
Address: American Federation of Teachers, AFL-CIO
555 New Jersey Ave. N.W.
Washington, DC 20001
Telephone: (202) 879-4400
Website: http://www.aft.org/benefits/scholarships/eligibility.cfm

---

American Institute for Foreign Study (AIFS) International Scholarship

---

Overview: Each semester AIFS offers 40 scholarships of $1,000 to students who demonstrate high academic achievement and write an essay addressing "How study abroad will impact my academic and personal growth."

Eligibility Requirements: Applicants must submit the AIFS scholarship application, the program application, the required application fee of $95, official transcripts of all college records to date and an academic reference. Completed scholarship and program applications must be postmarked by April 15th for Academic Year/Fall Quarter/Fall Semester or September 15th for Spring Quarter/Spring Semester. Students must meet the minimum requirements for the program to which they are applying, have at least a 3.0 minimum cumulative GPA, show leadership potential and be involved in extracurricular activities centered on multicultural or international issues.

Amount:	(40) $1,000 awards
Deadline:	*Fall/April 15th *Spring/September 15th
Address:	AIFS College Division
	River Plaza
	9 West Broad Street
	Stamford, CT 06902
Contact:	info@aifs.com
Telephone:	1-800-727-2437
Fax:	(203) 399-5597
Website:	http://www.aifsabroad.com/scholarships.asp

Banks Family Scholarships

Overview: Cynthia Banks, CEO of GlobaLinks Learning Abroad, and her family have personally donated an annual scholarship through the Foundation for Global Scholars in support of education abroad for future leaders and in particular for students in business and entrepreneurship. Cynthia was a business student and an entrepreneur who founded the GlobaLinks Learning Abroad organization in 1989. "Our family wishes to support students in their international endeavors so that they also have similar opportunities to explore their interests and career passions," said Cynthia Banks.

Eligibility Requirements: At the time of applying for any of the Foundation scholarships, you must be enrolled in a North American college or university where transfer credit from an academic program abroad will be applied to your degree being earned. (The exception to this requirement is the GlobaLinks Learning Abroad Internship Scholarship. There are no other exceptions.) You must be a US or Canadian citizen. In addition applicants must meet all of the following eligibility requirements for this award: have a minimum 3.0 GPA, be a business Major, be a GlobaLinks learning abroad student, have a interest in entrepreneurship and be attending a semester abroad program only and answer one additional essay question on the scholarship application.

Amount:	$1,000
Deadline:	Varies by semester of study
Address:	The Foundation for Global Scholars
	Banks Family Scholarship
	12050 N. Pecos St.
	Suite 320
	Westminster, CO 80234
Contact:	kbrockwell@foundationforglobalscholars.org
Telephone:	(303) 502-7256
Website:	http://www.foundationforglobalscholars.org/ Scholarships

The Beinecke Scholarship Program

Overview: The Beinecke Scholarship Program was established in 1971 by the Board of Directors of The Sperry and Hutchinson Company to honor Edwin, Frederick, and Walter Beinecke. The Board created an endowment to provide substantial scholarships for the graduate education of young men and women of exceptional promise. The program seeks to encourage and enable highly motivated students to pursue opportunities available to them and to be courageous in the selection of a graduate course of study in the arts, humanities and social sciences. Since 1975, the program has selected more than 490 college juniors from more than 100 different undergraduate institutions for support during graduate study at any accredited university. Each scholar receives $4,000 immediately prior to entering graduate school and an additional $30,000 while attending graduate school. There are no geographic restrictions on the use of the scholarship, and recipients are allowed to supplement the award with other scholarships, assistantships and research grants. Scholars are encouraged to begin graduate study as soon as possible following graduation from college, and must utilize all of the funding within five years of completion of undergraduate studies.

Eligibility Requirements: Applicants must have demonstrated superior standards of intellectual ability, scholastic achievement and personal promise during his or her undergraduate career, be a college junior pursuing a bachelor's degree during the current academic year. "Junior" means a student who plans to continue full-time undergraduate study and who expects to receive a baccalaureate degree between December 2012 and August 2013, plan to enter a master's or doctoral program in the arts, humanities or social sciences. Students in the social sciences who plan to pursue graduate study in neuroscience should not apply for a Beinecke Scholarship, be a United States citizen or a United States national from American Samoa or the Commonwealth of the Northern Mariana Islands.

Amount:	$34,000 total - $4,000 prior to entry of program & $30,000 while attending program
Deadline:	March 1st
Address:	Thomas L. Parkinson, Ph.D.
	Program Director
	8240 Peach Lane
	Fogelsville, PA 18051
Contact:	BeineckeScholarship@earthlink.net
Telephone:	(610) 395-5560
Website:	http://foundationcenter.org/grantmaker/beinecke/

Boren Undergraduate Scholarship

Overview: Boren Scholarships provide up to $20,000 to U.S. undergraduate students to study abroad in areas of the world that are critical to U.S. interests and underrepresented in study abroad, including Africa, Asia, Central & Eastern Europe, Eurasia, Latin America, and the Middle East. The countries of Western Europe, Canada, Australia, and New Zealand are excluded. Boren Scholars represent a variety of academic backgrounds, but all are interested in studying less commonly taught languages, including but not limited to Arabic, Chinese, Korean, Portuguese, Russian, and Swahili. . For a complete list of countries and languages to study please see the website.

Eligibility Requirements: Applicants must be a U.S. citizen at the time of application, high school graduate, or have earned a GED, matriculated in an undergraduate degree program located within the United States accredited by an accrediting body recognized by the U.S. Department of Education. Boren Scholars must remain matriculated in their undergraduate programs for the duration of the scholarship and may not graduate until the scholarship is complete, applying to a study abroad program that meets home institution standards in a country outside of Western Europe, Canada, Australia, or New Zealand. Boren Scholarships are not for study in the United States.

Amount:	Summer/$8,000, Semester/$10,000, Academic year/$20,000
Deadline:	January 31st
Address:	Boren Scholarships and Fellowships Institute of International Education 1400 K Street, NW, 7th Floor Washington, DC 20005-2403
Contact:	boren@iie.org, Christopher Powers Director, Boren Scholarships, and Fellowships
Telephone:	1-800-618- 6737
Fax:	(202) 326-7672
Website:	http://www.borenawards.org/boren_scholarship/basics.html

Boren Fellowship

Overview: Boren Fellowships provide up to $30,000 to U.S. graduate students to add an important international and language component to their graduate education through specialization in area study, language study, or increased language proficiency. Boren Fellowships support study and research in areas of the world that are critical to U.S. interests, including Africa, Asia, Central & Eastern Europe, Eurasia, Latin America, and the Middle East. The countries of Western Europe, Canada, Australia, and New Zealand are excluded. Boren Fellows represent a variety of academic and professional disciplines, but all are interested in studying less commonly taught languages, including but not limited to Arabic, Chinese, Korean, Portuguese, Russian and Swahili. For a complete list of countries and languages to study please see the website.

Eligibility Requirements: Applicants must be A U.S. citizen at the time of application, have either matriculated in or applying to a graduate degree program at a U.S. college or university located within the United States and accredited by an accrediting body recognized by the U.S. Department of Education. Boren Fellows must remain matriculated in their graduate programs for the duration of the fellowship and may not graduate until the fellowship is complete, be planning an overseas program that meets home institution standards in a country outside of Western Europe, Canada, Australia, or New Zealand. Boren Fellowships are not for study in the United States.

Amount:	Up to $30,000
Deadline:	February 9th
Address:	Boren Scholarships and Fellowships
	Institute of International Education
	1400 K Street, NW, 7th Floor
	Washington, DC 20005-2403
Contact:	boren@iie.org, Christopher Powers Director,
	Boren Scholarships, and Fellowships
Telephone:	1-800-618- 6737
Fax:	(202) 326-7672
Website:	http://www.borenawards.org/boren_fellowship

Chafee Grant

Overview: If you are or were in foster care and have financial need, you may qualify for up to $5,000 a year for career and technical training or college. You don't have to pay this money back. You may also be able to use your grant to help pay for childcare, transportation and rent while you're in school. You can use your Chafee Grant at any eligible California college or university or career or technical school, as well as schools in other states.

Eligibility Requirements: To qualify, you must be a current or former foster youth and not have reached your 22nd birthday as of July 1 of the award year. The court must have established your dependency when you were between the ages of 16 and 18. (KinGap youth, adopted youth, guardian placement, and voluntary placement may not be eligible for the Chafee Grant, unless court dependence was established, at anytime, between the ages of 16 and 18). The California Department of Social Services will verify your foster youth eligibility status.

Amount:	$5,000
Deadline:	July 1st
Address:	California Student Aid Commission
	Specialized Programs Operations Branch
	California Chafee Grant Program
	P.O. Box 419029
	Rancho Cordova, CA 95741-9029
Telephone:	1-888-224-7268
Website:	https://www.chafee.csac.ca.gov/default.aspx

College Jumpstart Scholarship

Overview: The College JumpStart Scholarship is an annual, merit-based competition -- financial need is not considered -- open to 10th -12th graders, college students, and non-traditional students.

Eligibility Requirements: Applicants must be a high school 10th-12th grader, college student or non-traditional student; U.S. citizen or legal resident; attend or plan to attend an accredited 2-year, 4-year or vocational / trade school in the U.S; be committed to using education to better your life and that of your family and/or community.

Amount:	1st place $1,500 scholarship, 2nd place $750 scholarship, Honorable Mentions $250 scholarships
Deadline:	October 17th and April 15th of each year
Address:	College JumpStart Scholarship
	c/o College JumpStart Scholarship Fund

4546 B10 El Camino Real No. 325
Los Altos, California 94022
Contact: admin@jumpstart-scholarship.net
Website: http://www.jumpstart-scholarship.net/

Congressional Black Caucus (CBC) Cheerios Brand Health Initiative Scholarship

Overview: This scholarship program focusing on health was established in 1998 as the CBC partnered with the naming sponsor, General Mills, to increase the number of minority students pursuing degrees in the fields of medicine, engineering, technology, nutrition and other health-related professions. Since the inception of the program, General Mills has invested more than $1,000,000 to underwrite this initiative. The CBC Spouses Cheerio's Brand Health Initiative Scholarship has served hundreds of students over the years, and has helped to create leaders in the medical and health related fields.

Eligibility Requirements: Applicants must be preparing to pursue an undergraduate or graduate degree full-time or be a current full-time student in good academic standing at an accredited college or university. Be planning to pursue a degree in the fields of medicine, engineering, technology, nutrition, or other health-related studies. Have a minimum 2.5 GPA. Exhibit leadership ability and participate in community service activities. *Preference will be given to CBC member constituents.

Amount: $5,000
Deadline: May 31st
Address: CBC Spouses Cheerio's Brand Health Initiative Scholarship
1720 Massachusetts Ave. NW
Washington, DC 20036
Contact: scholarships@cbcfinc.org
Telephone: (202) 263-2800
Fax: (202) 775-0773
Website: http://www.cbcfinc.org/cbcs-cheerios

Congressional Black Caucus (CBC) Louis Stokes Health Scholars Program

Overview: The Louis Stokes Health Scholars program, sponsored by the United Health Foundation, seeks to increase the number of qualified, yet underrepresented, college students entering the health workforce. Preference will be given to students who demonstrate an interest to work in underserved communities. Students currently attending two-year institutions are strongly encouraged to apply.

Eligibility Requirements: Applicants must be U.S. citizens or legal U.S. residents who have a minimum 3.0 GPA on a 4.0 scale. Applicants must also be currently enrolled or planning to enroll in a full-time undergraduate course of study at an accredited two- or four-year college, university, or technical school. The anticipated degree must be in a subject that will lead to a career in a health field. The ideal candidate is a student at a two-year institution who plans to complete a four-year degree and seek work in an underserved community. Additionally, the candidate will demonstrate financial need. Employees or immediate family members of UnitedHealth Group and its affiliates, CBC Members, the CBC Foundation staff, the CBC Foundation Board of Directors or the CBC Foundation Corporate Advisory Council are not eligible.

Amount:	(10) $8,000
Deadline:	March 29th
Address:	Louis Stokes Health Scholars Program
	Congressional Black Caucus Foundation, Inc.
	1720 Massachusetts Ave. NW
	Washington, DC 20036
Contact:	scholarships@cbcfinc.org
Telephone:	(202) 263-2800
Fax:	(202) 775-0773
Website:	http://www.cbcfinc.org/scholarships.html

Congressional Black Caucus (CBC) Environmental Studies Scholarship

Overview: The Environmental Studies Scholarship seeks to provide financial awards to minority and women college students pursuing a degree in environmental science or other related fields of study. Applicants should have a junior class standing in college with a declared major in environmental science or a related field, and understanding and acceptance of ServiceMaster's core values which allow people to be their best serving others.

Eligibility Requirements: Applicants must be U.S. citizens or legal U.S. residents who have a minimum 2.5 GPA on a 4.0 scale. Applicants must also be currently enrolled in a full-time undergraduate course of study at an accredited four-year college or university. The anticipated degree must be in a subject that will lead to an environmental career. The ideal candidate is a student at an accredited institution who plans to complete a four-year degree and seek work in an underserved community. Additionally, the candidate will demonstrate understanding and acceptance of ServiceMaster's core values. Employees or immediate family members of ServiceMaster's and its brands, CBC Members, staff of CBC Members, the CBC Foundation staff, the CBC Foundation Board of Directors or the CBC Foundation Corporate Advisory Council are not eligible.

Amount:	(2) $5,000 per semester
Deadline:	March 29th
Address:	Environmental Studies Scholarship
	Congressional Black Caucus Foundation, Inc.
	1720 Massachusetts Ave. NW
	Washington, DC 20036
Contact:	scholarships@cbcfinc.org
Telephone:	(202) 263-2800
Fax:	(202) 775-0773
Website:	http://www.cbcfinc.org/scholarships.html

Congressional Black Caucus (CBC) Spouses Heineken USA Performing Arts Scholarship

Overview: Established in the year 2000, the CBC Spouses Heineken USA Performing Arts scholarship program was developed in honor of the late Curtis Mayfield to ensure that students pursuing a career in the performing arts receive the financial assistance to achieve their goals. The performing arts include drama, music, dance, opera, marching bands and other musical ensembles.

Eligibility Requirements: Applicants must be preparing to pursue an undergraduate degree full-time or be a current full-time student in good academic standing at an accredited college or university. Be planning to pursue a degree in a field that will lead to a career in the performing arts. Have a minimum 2.5 GPA. Exhibit leadership ability and participate in community service activities.

Amount:	(10) $3,000
Deadline:	May 3rd
Address:	CBC Spouses Heineken USA Performing Arts Scholarship
	Congressional Black Caucus Foundation, Inc.
	1720 Massachusetts Ave. NW
	Washington, DC 20036
Contact:	scholarships@cbcfinc.org
Telephone:	(202) 263-2800
Fax:	(202) 775-0773
Website:	http://www.cbcfinc.org/scholarships.html

Davis Putter Scholarship Fund

Overview: The Davis-Putter Scholarship Fund provides grants to students actively working for peace and justice. These need-based scholarships are awarded to those able to do academic work at the university level and who are a part of the progressive movement on the campus and in the community. Early recipients worked for civil rights, against McCarthyism, and for peace in Vietnam. Recent grantees have been active in the struggle against racism, sexism, homophobia, and other forms of oppression; building the movement for economic justice; and creating peace through international anti-imperialist solidarity.

Eligibility Requirements: Applicants must include a short personal statement. Transcripts. Letters of support from two people able to evaluate the applicant's current political work, an official financial statement (i.e., FAFSA or SAR), and a passport-like photograph suitable for reproduction. Although citizenship is not a consideration, applicants must be living in the United States and planning to enroll in school in the US in order to apply. There is a strong preference for grantees who plan on staying in the US and building the movement here. The maximum grant is $10,000 and may be considerably smaller depending on the applicant's circumstances and the amount of funding available. Davis-Putter scholars are both graduate and undergraduate students and must be enrolled in an accredited school and receiving college credit for the time period covered by their grant. Completed applications must be postmarked.

Amount:	Up to $10,000
Deadline:	April 1st
Address:	Davis-Putter Scholarship Fund
	Post Office Box 7307
	New York, NY 10116
Contact:	administrator@davisputter.org
Website:	http://www.davisputter.org

Dolphin Scholarship Foundation

Overview: Dolphin Scholarship Foundation grants are available, on a competitive basis, to high school or college children/stepchildren of:

(1) Members or former members of the Submarine Force who have qualified in submarines and have served in the Submarine Force for at least eight years; or of

(2) Navy members who have served in submarine support activities (e.g., submarine bases, tenders, and rescue vessels) for a

minimum of ten years. These years of service need not be consecutive. Qualifying time must have been served on active duty; time served as a Naval Academy or NROTC midshipman, in "Boot Camp", or as a member of the inactive or Selected Naval Reserve cannot be used to establish eligibility. The time in service requirement may be waived for qualified submariners who have been medically retired or medically discharged from the Navy due to injury or illness, which occurred in the line of duty. There is no minimum period of service for children of personnel who died while on active duty in the Submarine Force.

Eligibility Requirements: Applicants must be a high school senior or college student. Be a child or stepchild of a member or former member of the U.S. Navy Submarine Force. Be Unmarried on March 15th and under age 24 on March 15th of the application year. Attend a four year accredited college or university and intend to work toward a BS or BA degree.

Amount:	$3,400 annually, up to $13,600 over 8 semesters
Deadline:	March 15th
Address:	Dolphin Scholarship Foundation
	4966 Euclid Road
	Suite 109
	Virginia Beach, VA 23462
Contact:	scholars@dolphinscholarship.org
Telephone:	(757) 671-3200 ext. 111
Fax:	(757) 671-3330
Website:	https://www.dolphinscholarship.org/

Foreclosure.com Scholarship Program

Overview: Foreclosure.com has issued $27,000 in scholarship money to 15 college students nationwide since the program was introduced in 2009. Each year, the company challenges future leaders of America to provide creative solutions/ideas to many of the nation's most critical issues, real estate/housing in particular, which can be used to help turnaround the market. With the presidential election looming in 2012, the hot-button housing/foreclosure issue will be the subject of great debate. And it's our goal to showcase the best plans for recovery that can truly make a difference moving forward.

Eligibility Requirements: Currently enrolled college students are invited to apply by submitting an essay. Freshman entering the fall semester are eligible once they have received a student ID number.

Requirements: Minimum 800 words, Maximum 2,000. Graduate students, law students, and/or high school seniors are NOT eligible)

Amount:	Five winners will be selected. Top prize $5,000, 2nd - 5th place will receive $1,000 each
Deadline:	December 1st
Address:	Foreclosure Free Search Inc.
	2201 NW Corporate Blvd #200
	Boca Raton, FL 33431
Contact:	scholarship@foreclosure.com
Telephone:	(561) 988-9669 ext. 7387
Website:	http://www.foreclosure.com/scholarship

Frame My Future Scholarship Contest

Overview: The "Frame My Future" Scholarship Contest is not your typical chance to win scholarship money for school there are no long forms to fill out or an extensive list of requirements that you need to meet. It's meant to be a fun and creative way to earn scholarship money!

Eligibility Requirements: Applicants must create an original entry piece that shares with us what you want to achieve in your personal and professional life after college. Follow the theme: This is how I "Frame My Future." Your creation must be submitted through the online entry form, within one image, in a .JPG or .PNG format, and must be fully viewable and/or readable online. The entry form also includes a section to submit a short accompanying description of your entry piece (maximum of 500 characters).

Amount:	(5) $1,000, plus $1,000 donation to grand prize winner's college's general endowment fund, on behalf of the grand prize winner.
Deadline:	March 2nd
Address:	Frame My Future Scholarship Contest Church Hill Classics 594 Pepper Street Monroe, CT 06468
Contact:	info@diplomaframe.com
Telephone:	1-800-477-9005, (203) 268-1535
Fax:	(203) 268-2468
Website:	http://www.diplomaframe.com/contests/frame-my-future-scholarship-contest-2011.aspx

GE Foundation/LULAC Scholarship Program

Overview: The General Electric Foundation/League of United Latin American Citizens (LULAC) Scholarship Program is intended to assist and encourage outstanding minority students in completing their college education. The program is directed specifically to disadvantaged minority students with career interests in business or engineering. The GE/LULAC Scholarship Program is sponsored by the General Electric Foundation and is administered by the LULAC National Educational Service Centers (LNESC), the educational branch of LULAC. All awards are contingent upon the support of the General Electric Foundation.

Eligibility Requirements: Applicants must be a minority student pursuing full-time studies leading to a bachelor's degree at an accredited college or university in the U.S.

- Must be CLASSIFIED AS A COLLEGE SOPHOMORE in the fall semester.
- Must have a cumulative college grade point average of at least 3.25 on a 4.0 scale or the equivalent.
- Must be a business or engineering major.
- Must be a U.S. citizen or legal resident.

Amount:	$5,000
Deadline:	August 10th
Address:	Applications are only accepted via mail to local participating LULAC Councils in the state or community in which the applicant resides. (Find your local LULAC council.) See website for local chapters.
Contact:	scholarships@lnesc.org
Telephone:	(202) 835-9646 Ext. 114
Website:	www.lnesc.org/

Gen and Kelly Tanabe Scholarship

Overview: The Gen and Kelly Tanabe Scholarship is a merit-based program that helps students fulfill their dreams of a higher education. The scholarship is named for Gen and Kelly Tanabe, best-selling authors on education, whose generous donations fund this program. Winners are chosen by committee, which bases its decision primarily on the submitted personal statement. The first place award is a $1,000 scholarship. The award can be used for tuition, room and board, required fees or any educational expense.

Eligibility Requirements: Applicants must be 9th-12th grade high school, college, or graduate student including adult students; legal resident of the U.S. currently in school or planning to start school within the next 12 months.

Amount:	$1,000
Deadline:	Fall December 31st Spring July 31st
Address:	Gen and Kelly Tanabe Student Scholarship
	3286 Oak Court
	Belmont, CA 94002
Contact:	scholarships@gkscholarship.com
Telephone:	(650) 618-2221
Website:	http://www.gkscholarship.com/

General Mills Technology Scholars Award

Overview: General Mills and UNCF have partnered to offer the General Mills Technology Scholars Award which provides a $5,000 scholarship for each academic year. Students will be selected based on academic performance, career aspirations, demonstrated leadership, and achievement. New applications are available in the spring of each year.

Eligibility Requirements: Designed for the student that is enrolled in a college or university for at least 2 to 4 years; the General Mills Technology Scholars Award is available to students majoring in certain fields like engineering and computer science.

Amount:	$5,000
Deadline:	April 30th
Address:	The United Negro College Fund
	Scholarships & Grants Administration
	8260 Willow Oaks Corporate Drive
	Fairfax, Virginia 22031
Contact:	rebecca.bennett@uncf.org
Telephone:	1-800-331-2244
Website:	www.uncf.org

General Mills Corporate Scholars Award
(The United Negro College Fund)

Overview: This General Mills Scholarship award offers $5,000 for the chosen applicant. It is a scholarship based on need. Applications are accepted through March 15th of the current school year.

Eligibility Requirements: The criteria for this award will be based upon the students' performance academically, career desires, the leadership they have demonstrated in school and in their community, and achievement. This General Mills scholarship is available to all undergraduates majoring in Business, Finance, Accounting, Marketing, Economics, human resources, supply chain management, operations management. Major in Business, Finance, Accounting, Marketing, Economics,

Human Resources, Supply Chain Management or Operations Management.

Amount: $5,000
Deadline: March 15th
Address: The United Negro College Fund
                 Scholarships & Grants Administration
                 8260 Willow Oaks Corporate Drive
                 Fairfax, Virginia 22031
Contact: rebecca.bennett@uncf.org
Telephone: 1-800-331-2244
Website: www.uncf.org

GlobaLinks Learning Abroad Internship Scholarships

Overview: GlobaLinks Learning abroad is the international education leader in the facilitation of high quality international internships. In addition, we also offer a wide range of other international education programming such as semester/year abroad, short courses, and degree programs. GlobaLinks Learning Abroad understands the importance for students to build and explore careers early and often, not only domestically but in a global context as well. Investing in these types of experiences will help set students on the right professional path by the time they graduate.

Eligibility Requirements: At the time of applying for any of the Foundation scholarships, you must be enrolled in a North American college or university where transfer credit from an academic program abroad will be applied to your degree being earned. (The exception to this requirement is the GlobaLinks Learning Abroad Internship Scholarship. There are no other exceptions.)

You must be a US or Canadian citizen; Minimum GPA 3.0; recipients are required to blog throughout their internship and send their blog to GlobaLinks Learning Abroad; must be participating in an internship program through GlobaLinks Learning Abroad Students only and recipients must also participate in a post experience webinar on Career Development through GlobaLinks Learning Abroad.

Amount:	$1,000
Deadline:	Varies by semester of study (See deadline chart on website)
Address:	The Foundation for Global Scholars
	GlobaLinks Learning Abroad
	Internship Scholarship
	12050 N. Pecos St. Suite 320
	Westminster, CO 80234
Contact:	kbrockwell@foundationforglobalscholars.org
Telephone:	(303) 502-7256
Website:	http://www.foundationforglobalscholars.org/scholarships

The Google Anita Borg Memorial Scholarship: USA

Overview: Dr. Anita Borg devoted her adult life to revolutionizing the way we think about technology and dismantling barriers that keep women and minorities from entering computing and technology fields. Her combination of technical expertise and fearless vision continues to inspire and motivate countless women to become active participants and leaders in creating technology. In her honor, Google is proud to honor Anita's memory and support women in technology with the Google Anita Borg Memorial Scholarship. Google hopes to encourage women to excel in computing and technology and become active role models and leaders in the field. A group of female undergraduate and graduate students will be chosen from the applicant pool, and scholarships will be awarded based on the strength of each candidate's academic background and demonstrated leadership. All scholarship recipients and finalists will be invited to attend the Annual Google Scholars' Retreat.

Eligibility Requirements: Applicants must be a female student entering her senior year of undergraduate study or be enrolled in a graduate program in the current academic year at a university in the United States; Be enrolled in Computer Science or Computer

Engineering program, or a closely related technical field as a full-time student for the current academic year; Maintain a cumulative GPA of at least 3.5 on a 4.0 scale or 4.5 on a 5.0 scale or equivalent in your current program.

Amount:	$10,000
Deadline:	February 12th
Contact:	anitaborgscholarship@google.com
Website:	http://www.google.com/anitaborg/us/, http://www.google.com/anitaborg/us/first-years.html

Harry S. Truman Scholarship

Overview: The mission of the Truman Scholarship Foundation is to find and recognize college juniors with exceptional leadership potential who are committed to careers in government, the non-profit or advocacy sectors, education or elsewhere in the public service and to provide them with financial support for graduate study, leadership training, and fellowship with other students who are committed to making a difference through public service.

Eligibility Requirements: At the time they apply applicants must be a full-time student pursuing a bachelor's degree with junior-level academic standing; have senior-level standing in their third year of college enrollment; or a senior and a resident of Puerto Rico, the Virgin Islands, or a Pacific Island. Note: Students who have completed their bachelor's degree or are already attending graduate school are not eligible for the Truman Scholarship.

Amount:	(60-65) awards up to $30,000
Deadline:	Check with your college or university faculty representative for deadlines.
Address:	Harry S. Truman Scholarship 712 Jackson Place NW Washington, DC 20006
Contact:	office@truman.gov
Fax:	(202) 395-6995
Website:	http://truman.gov/for-candidates/how-to-become

Twitter: @KevBrown1 | Facebook.com/KevBrown001

a-truman-scholar

Institute of International Education National Security Education Program (Need Based Financial Aid Scholarships)

Overview: Freeman-ASIA (Freeman Awards for Study in Asia) is designed to support American undergraduates with demonstrated financial need who are planning to study overseas in East or Southeast Asia. The program's goal is to increase the number of Americans with first-hand exposure to and understanding of Asia and its peoples and cultures. Award recipients are required to share their experiences with their home campuses or communities to encourage study abroad by others and fulfill the program's goal of increasing understanding of Asia in the United States.

Eligibility Requirements: Applicants must be a U.S. citizen or permanent resident at the time of application for financial assistance to participate in the proposed study abroad program. The applicant is required to submit the Expected Family Contribution (EFC) figure, calculated through FAFSA, with the statement of financial need through the online Freeman-ASIA application. Must be an undergraduate student in good standing, pursuing his or her first bachelor's degree (or associate's degree), at a two-year or a four-year institution of higher education in the United States. Must apply through the U.S. home campus and have at least one term of enrollment remaining at the home institution in the U.S. upon returning from studying abroad in Asia. Must have applied or have been accepted to a study abroad based program in: Cambodia, China, Hong Kong, Indonesia, Japan, Korea, Laos, Macao, Malaysia, Mongolia, Philippines, Singapore, Taiwan, Thailand, and Vietnam.

A multi-country program is eligible only if the applicant will spend at least 8 weeks in one of the countries stated above and will have intensive language study during that period. Must have applied to or have been accepted by a study abroad based program that awards academic credits through the home campus or other U.S. accredited college or university. The proposed length of study in the host country must be a minimum of 8 weeks for a summer term, 10 weeks for a quarter term, and 12 weeks for a semester term. Must have little or no previous experience in the country in which he or she plans to study. A summer term applicant must not have spent more than 4 weeks in the proposed country of study within the last 5 years.

A semester or an academic year term applicant must not have spent more than 6 weeks in the proposed country of study within the last 5 years. Must submit the online Freeman-ASIA Student Impact Survey within one month of returning to the United States and must initiate his/her service project to promote study abroad opportunities in Asia on the college campus and/or in the local community. Must submit the Freeman-ASIA Final Service Report on the implementation of his/her service project at the end of the term following his/her return to the United States. Must not be a previous Freeman-ASIA award recipient.

Amount:	Summer/$3,000, Semester/Quarter $5,000, Full academic year $7,000
Deadline:	Student: Fall April 4th, Spring Oct.12th, Summer February 15th
	Advisor: Fall April 11th, Spring October 19th Summer February 22nd
Address:	Freeman-ASIA
	U.S. Student Programs
	Institute of International Education
	809 United Nations Plaza
	New York, NY 10017-3580
Contact:	Freeman-ASIA@iie.org
Telephone:	(212) 984-5542
Fax:	(212) 984-5325
Website:	http://www.iie.org/Programs/Freeman-ASIA

The IFDA Educational Foundation Green/Sustainable Design Scholarship

Overview: Aware of increasing environmental concerns worldwide, the IFDA Educational Foundation established a new scholarship for a student focusing on the evolving green/sustainable field of study. Sustainable design is the development of innovative ways to create living spaces that are energy efficient and feature green/sustainable materials, fabrications and products. The student applying for this scholarship is planning to become an educated participant in the green movement. Paying equal attention to both sustainability factors and design aesthetics, the student should be demonstrating creative use of green products and eco-friendly furnishings in class projects. The student is familiar with current information in the green/sustainable field, is applying this knowledge in class work, and has a goal of seeking a future LEED (Leadership in Energy and Environmental Design) accreditation.

Eligibility Requirements: Applicants must have completed the application and have completed four design courses in post-secondary education at the time of applying and are majoring in Interior Design or a closely related field. The completed application packet must include: A sealed transcript of course work that verifies full-time status with your GPA. (May be sent separately.) And four (4) copies each the following:

- The completed Application Form
- A 200-400 word essay explaining your long and short-term goals, extracurricular activities, volunteer work, and what led you to pursue a career in this field
- Copies of two to three different examples of your original design work featuring aspects of green/sustainable design with detailed explanations (digital color copies preferred or CD)
- Letter of Recommendation from a professor or instructor on official school stationery

Amount: $1,500
Deadline: March 31st
Address: IFDA/EF Director of Scholarships & Grants:
Sue Williams, Colleagues,
2700 East Grace Street,
Richmond, VA 23223

Contact: colleaguesinc@earthlink.net
Telephone: 804-644-3946
Fax: 804-644-3834
Website: http://www.ifdaef.org/scholarships.php

The IFDA Educational Foundation Part time Student Scholarship

Overview: The IFDA Educational Foundation Board of Trustees have added a scholarship for a part time undergraduate student enrolled in a continuing interior design or related program at an accredited school.

Eligibility Requirements: Applicants must have completed four design courses in post-secondary education at the time of application and be majoring in Interior Design or a related field; the scholarship applicant must be currently enrolled in at least two courses as a part-time student. The completed application packet must include a sealed transcript of course work that verifies part-time status and shows your GPA. Transcript may be sent separately.

Amount: $1,500
Deadline: March 31st
Address: Merry Mabbett Dean, FIFDA,
                   Director of Grants
                   10765 SW Canterbury Lane, #101,
                   Tigard, OR 97224
Contact: merrymabbettinc@comcast.net
Telephone: (503) 367-0151
Fax: 1-866-362-9107
Website: http://www.ifdaef.org/scholarships.php

Jack Kent Cooke Foundation Undergraduate Transfer Scholarships

Overview: The Jack Kent Cooke Foundation's Undergraduate Transfer Scholarship honors excellence by supporting outstanding community college students with financial need to transfer to and complete their bachelor's degrees at the nation's top four-year colleges and universities.

Eligibility Requirements: Applicant must be a current student at an accredited U.S. community college or two-year institution with sophomore status by December 31, 2011, or a recent graduate (since spring 2007); plan to enroll full-time in a baccalaureate program at an accredited college or university in fall 2012; have a cumulative undergraduate grade-point average of 3.50 or better on a scale of 4.0 (or the equivalent); be nominated by the Jack Kent Cooke Foundation Faculty Representative at his or her two-year institution; have significant unmet financial need; have not previously been nominated for the Jack Kent Cooke Foundation Undergraduate Transfer Scholarship;

While the Foundation considers academic excellence first in evaluating candidates, competitive applicants must also demonstrate unmet financial need, which has two components: Education costs that are appreciably greater than the total amount of other scholarships or grant awards and insufficient student and family income to meet educational costs.

Amount:	$30,000
Deadline:	December 6th
Address:	Jack Kent Cooke Foundation
	44325 Woodridge Parkway
	Lansdowne, Virginia 20176
Contact:	jkc@applyists.com
Telephone:	1-888-264-3062
Fax:	(703) 723-8030
Website:	http://www.jkcf.org/scholarships/undergraduate-transfer-scholarships/

J.W. Saxe Memorial Prize

Overview: The award is meant to enable the student to gain practical experience in public service by taking a no-pay or low-pay job or internship during a summer or other term. Preference will be given applicants who have already found such a position, but who require additional funds.

Eligibility Requirements: Applicant must be a undergraduate or graduate student in an accredited college or university; seeking support for an internship in public service, not general support; demonstrated public service activity -- past, present and/or future; financial need will be taken into consideration.

Amount:	$2,000
Deadline:	March 15th
Address:	J.W. Saxe Memorial Prize
	1524 31st Street
	Washington, DC 20007
Contact:	Ruth Saxe, President - ruthsaxe@aol.com or
	Elinor Sachse, VP and Secretary
	sachsedc@verizon.net
Website:	http://www.jwsaxefund.org

Leonard C. Ball and James H. Bell Scholarship

Overview: Each year the Coalition of Black Trade Unionists (CBTU) awards ten scholarships to high school and college students in the names of two men who exemplified union activism and a thirst for knowledge. The Leonard C. Ball and James H. Bell Scholarship Fund was established to honor the late Leonard Ball, the first executive director of CBTU and the top aide to AFSCME International Secretary Treasurer William Lucy, and the late Jim Bell, president of the New York Chapter of the Coalition of Black Trade Unionists and a major force in the city politics of New York City.

Eligibility Requirements: Scholarship-Students, CBTU members, who have or are about to graduate from high school and have applied or have already been accepted by a college or university, are eligible for this scholarship. Scholarship-Students, CBTU members, who are currently enrolled in a college or university, have completed their freshman year, with a minimum 2.5 grade point average, are eligible for this scholarship. Applicant must have written evidence of acceptance and or attendance at an accredited college/university. College Student must have a "C" average GPA among other criteria. This will be a determining factor in the selection process. Among other requirements, students must submit a typewritten essay of no less than 300 words.

Amount: (10) 2,000
Deadline: April 4th
Address: CBTU National Office
1150 17th Street, NW
Suite 300
Washington, DC 20036
Contact: cbtu1@hotmail.com
Telephone: (202) 778-3318
Fax: (202) 293-5308
Website: http://www.cbtu.org/bell%20ball.html

Leopold Schepp Foundation
(Undergraduate/Graduate Awards)

Overview: Leopold Schepp established the Foundation in 1925. His objectives were to encourage young people to develop good character and to help them complete their high school education, an opportunity he never had. In 1932, in recognition of the changes in a society that made a high school education universally available, the Foundation changed its focus to include young men and women pursuing full-time undergraduate and graduate study. The scope of the Foundation was further broadened following Miss Schepp's death in 1964 by a bequest she made for the purpose of establishing fellowships for post-doctoral study and research in specific fields.

Eligibility Requirements: Undergraduates must be under 30 years of age at the time of application. Graduates must be under 40 years of age at the time of application. Applicants must have a minimum GPA of 3.0 on a 4.0 scale and must enroll full-time. PhD candidates who have only the dissertation to complete and who are not enrolled in class full-time are not eligible. Only one student in a family can apply and receive a scholarship at the same time. High school seniors are eligible to apply during their senior year in high school for their first year in college. Applicants must be citizens or permanent residents of the United States. Scholars who are requesting aid for a second degree at the same level for which a degree has already been awarded are not eligible to apply, for example, a second Bachelor's Degree or second Master's Degree. Due to limited funding, the number of applications given to students enrolled in graduate study at medical, law or business school is limited. A personal interview in New York City is required of all applicants. Travel expenses are not reimbursed. Students who have previously applied for a Leopold Schepp Foundation Scholarship and who were denied an award are not eligible to reapply.

Amount:	Up to $8,500
Deadline:	Varies
Address:	The Leopold Schepp Foundation
	551 Fifth Avenue
	Suite 3000
	New York, NY 10176-3201
Telephone:	(212) 692-0191
Website:	http://www.scheppfoundation.org/wp/applying/

Lowrider Magazine: Adelante Raul Yzaguirre Scholarship

Overview: The Adelante Raul Yzaguirre Award recognizes individuals or organizations whose activist vision of equality advances the inclusion and progress of the Hispanic community.

Eligibility Requirements: Applicants must submit a 1-2 page essay (details on website). Must have a 2.5 GPA or higher. Must be currently enrolled in or accepted to a 2-yr or 4-yr college. Must provide a copy of most recent high school or college transcript. Must provide one (1) letter of recommendation from a college professor, guidance counselor, principal or other institutional leader. Essay: Students are invited to submit an essay (no more than 2 pages) answering one of the following questions: 1) What person or circumstance has most impacted your life? 2) What legacy do you wish to leave behind? 3) What specifically have you done to make a difference in your community?

Amount:	1st place $6,000, 2nd place $3,000, 3rd place $1,000
Deadline:	July 31st
Address:	Frito-Lay, Inc.
	c/o Jesus Diaz
	2465 Golden Bear Court
	Carrollton, TX 75006
Contact:	flnaadelante@pepsico.com
Website:	http://www.lowridermagazine.com/ hotnews/lrmp_1106_adelante_raul_yzaguirre_sc holarship_award/index.html

Malcolm X Scholarship for "Exceptional Courage"

Overview: The Malcolm X Scholarship is awarded to students who have overcome tremendous hardships and special circumstances.

Eligibility Requirements: The student must demonstrate academic excellence and involvement in the campus community. This renewable scholarship provides an award of $4,000 for a student attending one of United Negro College Fund member institutions.

Amount:	$4,000
Deadline:	May 5th
Address:	The United Negro College Fund
	Scholarships & Grants Administration
	8260 Willow Oaks Corporate Drive
	Fairfax, Virginia 22031
Telephone:	1-800-331-2244
Website:	http://www.uncf.org

Microsoft Academic United States University Scholarship

Overview: A Microsoft scholarship provides a leg up so you can pursue undergraduate studies in computer science and related technical disciplines. You'll join a community of scholarship recipients from the United States, Canada and Mexico who share your passion for technology and academic excellence. It all adds up to achieving your primary goal—making a real difference in the software industry.

Eligibility Requirements: To be eligible, you must be enrolled full time in a Bachelor's degree program at a 4-year college or university in the United States, Canada, or Mexico at the time you submit the application. Plus, we'll need to see that you're making satisfactory progress toward an undergraduate degree in computer science, computer engineering, or a related technical discipline such as electrical engineering, math, or physics—and that you demonstrate an interest in computer science. Because the scholarship is merit based, you must maintain a 3.0 cumulative grade point average out of a possible 4.0, or a 4.0 cumulative grade point average out of a possible 5.0. You will need to provide your
resume, transcript, answers to essay questions, letter of referral, Printed Confirmation Page from Online Application to the Microsoft Internship Program.

Amount:	Full and partial tuition scholarships
Deadline:	February 1st
Address:	Microsoft Scholarship Program
	Microsoft Corporation
	One Microsoft Way
	Redmond, WA 98052-8303
Contact:	scholars@microsoft.com
Website:	http://careers.microsoft.com/careers/
	en/us/internships-scholarships.aspx

NAACP National Office (Agnes Jones Jackson)

Overview: Each year the NAACP, through generous donations, is able to provide scholarships to outstanding students. It is the duty of our dedicated Scholarship Committee to determine the most outstanding individuals to receive these awards. The NAACP does not provide financial aid to individuals, only scholarships through this process.

Eligibility Requirements: Applicant must be a current member of the NAACP and must not have reached the age of 25 by the application deadline. Applicant must be a citizen of the United States and be enrolled in an accredited college or university in the United States. Undergraduate students must be full-time with a GPA of at least 2.5 (C+). Graduate students may be full or part-time with a GPA of 3.0 (B). Applicant must demonstrate financial need. Renewal of the Agnes Jones Jackson Scholarship is competitive.

Amount:	$1,500-$2,500
Deadline:	March 31st
Address:	National Association for the Advancement of Colored People (NAACP)
	4805 Mount Hope Drive
	Baltimore, MD 21215-3297
Contact:	adugger@naacpnet.org
Telephone:	(410) 580-5760
Fax:	(410) 585-1329
Website:	http://www.naacp.org/pages/naacp-scholarships, http://www.aie.org/scholarships/detail.cfm?id=298

National Federation of the Blind Scholarship Program

Overview: To recognize achievement by blind scholars, the National Federation of the Blind annually offers blind college students in the United States the opportunity to win one of thirty national scholarships.

Eligibility Requirements: Applicant must be legally blind (Must submit "CONFIRMATION OF LEGAL BLINDNESS" form – found on website) in both eyes, and must be residing in the United States, the District of Columbia, or Puerto Rico. Must be pursuing or planning to pursue a full-time, postsecondary course of study in a degree program at a United States institution in the current scholastic year, except that one scholarship may be given to a person employed full-time while attending school part-time.

Must participate in the entire NFB national convention and in all scheduled scholarship program activities. In addition to a scholarship, each winner will receive assistance to attend the National Federation of the Blind Annual Convention in July, providing an excellent opportunity for high-level networking with active blind persons in many different professions and occupations.

Amount:	(30) ranging from $3,000 to $12,000
Deadline:	March 31st
Address:	NFB Scholarship Program
	National Federation Of The Blind
	at Jernigan Place
	200 East Wells Street
	Baltimore, Maryland 21230
Contact:	scholarships@nfb.org
Telephone:	(410) 659-9314, extension 2415
Fax:	(410) 685-5653
Website:	http://www.nfb.org/nfb/
	scholarship_program.asp?SnID=1744925766

National Italian American Foundation

Overview: The National Italian American Foundation (NIAF) has
an education budget of about $1 million. The NIAF will award scholarships and grants to outstanding students in the summer for use during the following academic year. The awards will be made on the basis of academic merit and divided between two groups of students.

Eligibility Requirements:

General Category I: Italian American students who demonstrate outstanding potential and high academic achievements. Area of study: open.

General Category II: Those students from any ethnic background majoring or minoring in Italian language, Italian studies, Italian American studies or a related field, who demonstrate outstanding potential and high academic achievements.

*Each scholarship award can only cover tuition and university-provided room and board. Scholarship recipients are eligible for one year of scholarship support. Scholarship monies not used during one academic year are not transferable to the following academic year. Scholarship applicants and winners can and are encouraged to reapply in subsequent years.

Amount: $2,000-$12,000
Deadline: March 2nd
Address: National Italian American Foundation
1860 19th Street NW
Washington, DC 20009
Contact: scholarships@niaf.org
Telephone: (202) 387-0600
Fax: (202) 387-0800
Website: http://www.niaf.org/scholarships/about.asp

Orphan Foundation of America

Overview: These scholarships are awarded based on a combination of merit and need, and funding levels are determined based on cost of attendance and other resources.

Eligibility Requirements: Applicants must have been in public or private foster care for a minimum of 12 consecutive months at the time of their 18th birthday; OR have been adopted or placed into legal guardianship from foster care after their 16th birthday; OR they must have been orphaned for at least one year at the time of their 18th birthday; have been accepted into or expect to be accepted into an accredited, Pell-eligible college or other post-secondary school; be under the age of 25 on March 31st of the year in which they first apply; have been in foster care or orphaned while living in the United States. U.S. citizenship is not required.

Amount:	Up to $6,000
Deadline:	April 15th
Address:	Foster Care to Success
	21351 Gentry Drive
	Suite 130
	Sterling, VA 20166
Telephone:	(571) 203-0270
Fax:	(571) 203-0273
Website:	http://fc2success.org/

Phillips Foundation
(The Ronald Reagan College Leaders Scholarship Program)

Overview: This program is limited to undergraduate degree candidates at accredited, 4-year degree-granting institutions in the United States or its possessions who have successfully completed their first (or freshman) year and have begun their second (or sophomore) year of study.

Eligibility Requirements: Students may apply for a scholarship to be made available at the start of the third (or junior) year of study. Winners may apply for renewal for the fourth (senior) year of study. Students in their third (i.e., junior) year may apply for a one-time scholarship for the senior year. Students at two-year schools may apply as juniors for a one-time award for the senior year upon transfer to a four-year institution. Applicants also must be citizens of the United States.

Amount:	Up to $10,000 at the Trustees' discretion
Deadline:	January 17th
Address:	The Phillips Foundation
	Attn: Jeff Hollingsworth
	1 Massachusetts Avenue, NW, Suite 620
	Washington, DC 20001
Contact:	jhollingsworth@thephillipsfoundation.org
Telephone:	(202) 250-3887 ext. 628
Website:	http://www.thephillipsfoundation.org/#
	ronald_reagan_scholarships.cfm

Proofreading.com Scholarship Program

Overview: The Proof-Reading.com Scholarship Program awards one $1,500 scholarship each year.

Eligibility Requirements: Attend classes at an accredited four-year college or university in the U.S. Take a minimum of 12 semester units (you must be a full-time student). Be a legal resident of the U.S. or provide a valid green card. Maintain a cumulative grade point average (GPA) of at least 3.5. You must write a minimum of 1,500 words in reference to the provided topic. There is no maximum word count. The scholarship committee will focus on grammar and applicants' ability to present ideas clearly. Include a Works Cited page, with a minimum of three sources. The essay must follow the Modern Language Association (MLA) system for documenting sources, which is set forth in the *MLA Handbook for Writers of Research Papers*, 7th edition (New York: MLA, 2009). Submit your essay using the form on the website. Do not send your transcript unless it is requested.

Amount:	$1,500
Deadline:	July 1st
Address:	Proof-Reading, Inc.
	12 Geary Street, Suite 806
	San Francisco, California 94108-5720
Contact:	scholarships@proof-reading.com
Telephone:	1-866-433-4867
Website:	http://www.proof-reading.com/proof-reading_scholarship_program.asp

Ronald McDonald House Charity (RMHC) U.S. Scholarships

Overview: Unfortunately, many of those students can't afford to get the education of their dreams. We want these students to reach their full potential. To help them accomplish this, our network of U.S. Chapters, along with RMHC Global, offer scholarships to students in financial need who have demonstrated academic achievement, leadership and community involvement. Since 1985, more than $44 million in scholarships have been awarded.

Eligibility Requirements: If you're under the age of 21 with at least a 2.7 GPA and demonstrated financial need, the RMHC Scholars scholarship is a great fit! It honors your scholastic, community and work performance and is open to all students, regardless of race, color, creed, religion, sexual orientation, gender, disability, or national origin. Scholarship availability and amount vary by participating chapter.

Amount:	Varies, apply online and contact your corresponding local Ronald McDonald House Charities chapter for detailed information.
Deadline:	January 27th
Address:	Ronald McDonald House Charities One Kroc Drive Oak Brook, IL 60523
Contact:	info@rmhc.org
Telephone:	(630) 623-7048
Website:	http://www.aboutmcdonalds.com/mcd/students/scholarships.html, http://rmhc.org/what-we-do/rmhc-u-s-scholarships

Ruth Lilly Poetry Fellowships

Overview: The Poetry Foundation and POETRY magazine have five recipients each year. Among the largest awards offered to aspiring poets in the United States, the $15,000 scholarship prize is intended to encourage the further study and writing of poetry.

Eligibility Requirements: Writers who are U.S. citizens between the ages of 21 and 31 as of March 31st are eligible. Using the online submission system, submit 10 pages of poetry, a one-page writer's statement, and a list of publications by March 31st. There is no entry fee. Visit the website for the required entry form and complete guidelines.

Amount: $15,000
Deadline: March 31st
Address: Poetry Foundation
61 West Superior Street
Chicago, IL 60654
Contact: mail@poetryfoundation.org
Telephone: (312) 787-7070
Fax: (312) 787-6650
Website: http://www.poetryfoundation.org/
foundation/prizes_fellowship

The Santana M. and Joaqium S. Ventura Portuguese History Award Application

Overview: The Sons of Portugal Scholarship was established in 1965 with the primary objective of recognizing and rewarding academic excellence among students of Portuguese descent.

Eligibility Requirements: Applicants must be of Portuguese descent living at least one full year in Danbury or its surrounding areas. Applicant or his/her parent(s) must be an active member of at least one of the following organizations and/or its active groups: Portuguese Cultural Center or Immaculate Heart of Mary Parish, Danbury. Scholarships will be granted to any accredited educational institution up to a maximum of four years per recipient. Applicant must have completed First Year of college and is continuing with his or her education or be in Graduate School.

Amount: 1st place $3,000 2nd place $2,500, 3rd place
$2,000, 4th place $1,500, 5th place $1,000
Deadline: April 7th
Address: Danny Martins
℅ The Sons of Portugal Scholarship Committee
8 Wilkes Rd.
Danbury, CT 06811
Telephone: (203) 748-1278
Website: http://www.portugueseculturalcenter.com/
organizations/scholarship

Sara's Wish Foundation

Overview: Sara's Wish Foundation scholarships are awarded to extraordinary young women committed to making the world a better place by fully participating in it.

Eligibility Requirements: Applicants must have a commitment to public service; a strong record of scholarship; a history of leadership experience; a sincere interest in the work of Sara's Wish Foundation; a willingness to join with Sara's Wish Foundation in its ongoing efforts to improve safety awareness

Amount:	$1,000-1,500
Deadline:	January 1st
Address:	Sara's Wish Foundation
	23 Ash Lane
	Amherst, MA 01002
Contact:	info@saraswish.org
Telephone:	(413) 256-0914
Website:	http://www.saraswish.org/international_t ravel.htm

The Scholarships Roothbert Fund

Overview: The Roothbert Fund was created in 1958 by Albert and Toni Roothbert to help men and women in need of financial aid to further their education. The principal focus of The Fund is its Scholarships Program, through which it makes grants for undergraduate or graduate study at accredited colleges or universities. Scholarships may only be applied to study at an accredited institution based in the United States. The Fund seeks candidates who are "motivated by spiritual values," and works to foster fellowship among them.

The Fund is a small, nearly all-volunteer scholarship fund based in New York City, which awards yearly grants and works to foster fellowship among grant recipients. Once a year, the Fund accepts applications for grants, which include essays, transcripts and recommendations. From these written applications, the Fund identifies a group of finalists to be invited for a brief personal interview. On the basis of this interview, the Fund typically selects about 20 new scholarship recipients each year.

Eligibility Requirements: Roothbert Fund scholarships are open to all in the United States regardless of sex, age, color, nationality or religious background. While the Fund does not emphasize any particular form of religious practice or worship, it seeks to provide support to persons motivated by spiritual values. The Fund has awarded grants to persons entering a wide range of careers. However, preference will be given to those who can satisfy high scholastic requirements and are considering careers in education. For more information, applicants should read with care the founders prologue in the History and Mission of the Fund.

Amount:	Averaging $2,000-$3,000
Deadline:	January 31st
Address:	The Roothbert Fund, Inc.
	475 Riverside Drive
	Room 1830
	New York, NY 10115
Contact:	mail@roothbertfund.org
Telephone:	(212) 870-3116
Website:	http://www.roothbertfund.org/scholarships.php

Semester at Sea Presidential Scholarship

Overview: The Semester at Sea Presidential Scholars program was developed to identify and support extremely high-achieving students wishing to enhance their global perspective and better understand their vital role as a global citizen. These students are expected to understand and further the mission of ISE before, during, and after their participation in the program.

Eligibility Requirements: Open to all students

Amount:	Full Tuition
Deadline:	September 21st and April 22nd

Address:	Semester at Sea
	Presidential Scholarship Committee
	PO Box 400885, Charlottesville, VA 22904
Contact:	studentservices@semesteratsea.org
Telephone:	(800) 854-0195
Website:	http://www.semesteratsea.org/admission-and-aid/overview/financial-aid-scholarships.php

Sports Journalism Institute

Overview: Ten student journalists will be selected. Ideally, applicants should be college sophomores or juniors. Candidates will be selected on the basis of academic achievement, demonstrated interest in sports journalism as a career and excellence on the required essay. *Eligibility is not limited to journalism majors.

Eligibility Requirements: Applicants must submit a current college transcript. Two letters of recommendation. A professional-style photo (headshot). Up to seven writing samples or clips (photocopied on 8½ by 11-inch paper). An essay of no more than 500 words stating why he or she should be selected. Incomplete applications will not be accepted.

Amount:	(10) $500
Deadline:	November 14th
Address:	The Boston Globe,
	135 Morrissey Blvd.
	Boston, MA 02125
Contact:	Gregory Lee, glee@globe.com
Telephone:	(617) 929- 2840
Website:	http://sportsjournalisminstitute.org/blog/about-us/

STA Travel Scholar Award

Overview: STA Travel Inc. is a global travel specialist with 30 years experience helping students, teachers and young professionals travel the world. STA Travel offers a unique range of products with exclusive discounts on airfare, accommodations, tours, rail passes and more. Globally, STA Travel is present in 90 countries with 400 retail locations, sending over 6 million travelers away each year. "Our mission is to create opportunities for students and young adults to experience the world around them," said Kevin Jacobs, STA Travel's managing director. "This donation helps us achieve that mission and give deserving students the opportunity to study abroad where they can learn just as much about themselves as the world around them."

Eligibility Requirements: Applicants must_at the time of applying for any of the Foundation scholarships; you must be enrolled in a North American college or university where transfer credit from an academic program abroad will be applied to your degree being earned. (The exception to this requirement is the GlobaLinks Learning Abroad Internship Scholarship. There are no other exceptions.) You must be a US or Canadian citizen students should also have an academic major at their home university in one of the following areas in order to apply for the STA Travel Scholar Award (academic minors in these areas are *not* eligible): Photography, Film and Art, Travel and Tourism, International Business, International Studies or, Foreign Language

Amount:	$2,500
Deadline:	Varies by semester of study (See deadline table)
Address:	The Foundation for Global Scholars
	STA Travel Scholar Award
	12050 N. Pecos St.
	Suite 320
	Westminster, CO 80234
Contact:	kbrockwell@foundationforglobalscholars.org
Telephone:	(303) 502-7256
Website:	http://www.foundationforglobalscholars.org/ Scholarships

Union (Lucy Dalbiac Luard Scholarship)

Overview: Open to sophomore students pursuing a four-year degree at UNCF institutions, Hampton University, or Howard

University in all major fields of study.

Eligibility Requirements: Candidates must excel academically (minimum 3.0 GPA), and exhibit the maturity and independence necessary for study abroad.

Amount:	*All expenses*: tuition, room, board, book allowance and travel expenses for their junior academic year at a British university.
Deadline:	November 16th
Address:	The English-Speaking Union of the United States National Headquarters 144 East 39th Street New York NY 10016 Attn: International Programs
Contact:	info@esuus.org
Telephone:	(212) 818-1200
Fax:	(212) 867-4177
Website:	http://www.esuus.org/ Luard_Scholarship_Apply.htm

USA Today (All-USA College Academic Team)

Overview: USA TODAY honors outstanding students with the All-USA Academic Teams. The top twenty students selected for each of the All-USA First Teams will receive a $2,500 cash award, trophy and will receive extensive national recognition through coverage in USA TODAY and usatoday.com. Second and third teams are named and each receives certificates of achievement.

Eligibility Requirements: Applicants must be a legal resident of the U.S. or DC (excluding Puerto Rico), enrolled as a full-time student of at least junior standing in a state-accredited private or public college, and in good standing during the current school year. Only 1 entry per applicant.

Applicant may not have received a baccalaureate degree prior to the year applying. Other eligibility restrictions and qualifications apply. By entering, applicants must meet eligibility requirements and comply with the All-USA College Academic Team guidelines and qualifications.

Amount:	(20) $2,500
Deadline:	February 18th
Address:	USA TODAY
	7950 Jones Branch Dr.
	McLean, VA 22108-9995
Contact:	Carol Skalski, allstars@usatoday.com.
Telephone:	(703) 854-5890
Website:	http://www.usatoday.com/
	marketing/academic_teams/index.html

USA Today (All-USA Community College Academic Team-Phi Theta Kappa Honor Society)

Overview: USA TODAY's All-USA Community College Academic Team recognizes exceptional students at the nation's community colleges. Judges consider grades, academic rigor, growth and how well the students use their education to benefit their schools and communities. The program is administered by Phi Theta Kappa International Honor Society. Each school may nominate two students. Phi Theta Kappa notifies community college presidents about the program in September.

Eligibility Requirements: Applicants must be enrolled in a regionally accredited institution offering an associate degree program; Have completed at least 12 hours of coursework that may be applied to an associate degree (part-time students may be eligible); Generally have a grade point average of 3.5; Receive an invitation to membership from the chapter at the college; Be presently enrolled; Adhere to the moral standards of the society.

Amount:	$2,500
Deadline:	December 1st
Address:	USA TODAY
	7950 Jones Branch Dr.
	McLean, VA 22108-9995

Or
Phi Theta Kappa Honor Society
1625 Eastover Drive
Jackson, MS 39211

Contact: Carol Skalski, allstars@usatoday.com.
Telephone: (703) 854-5890
Website: http://www.ptk.org/become-a-member/scholarships/academic-teams

Women's Overseas Service League

Overview: Scholarship awards are based upon the decisions of the Scholarship Committee of the Women's Overseas Service League Board of Directors. Scholarships average $500.00 to $1000.00 annually and may be renewed for a second year if the recipient maintains and reports satisfactory progress as delineated in the scholarship award criteria.

Eligibility Requirements: Applicants must be women who are committed to advancement in military or other public service careers. Have demonstrated such commitment through life experiences. Have successfully completed a minimum of 12 semester (or 18 quarter) hours of study in any institution of higher education with a minimum 2.5 grade point average. Are admitted for study in an institution of higher learning in a program leading to an academic degree (Associate Degree or higher). The program may be professional or technical in nature. Agree to enroll for a minimum of six semester (or nine quarter) hours of study each academic period. Agree to maintain academic standards.

Amount: $500 to $1000
Deadline: March 1st
Address: Women's Overseas Service League
Scholarship Committee
PO Box 124
Cedar Knolls, NJ 07927-0124
Contact: kelsey@openix.com
Website: http://www.wosl.org/scholarships.htm

125 DORMITORY ESSENTIALS CHECKLIST*

It is easy to forget the small things when buying for your big move into your college dorm room.

Your school should provide you with a checklist, but often, the list is short and does not include all essential items. Every college is different and your needs, as well as what is acceptable in your dormitory, will vary from institution to institution. Be sure to only bring those things that you will actually use.

If you are attending college out of state, you don't have to take a lot with you because you can buy items when you arrive. It is also a good idea to purchase all necessities before your parent or guardian leaves. After all, it's better to spend their money than yours. To help you remember the essentials, here is a checklist of 125 things that you may need for your dormitory:

* This checklist is available for download on the book's website **www.mydebtfreecollege.com/resources**

125

DORMITORY ESSENTIALS CHECKLIST

DORM ROOM
- [ ] BED ACCESSORIES
- [ ] DECORATIONS
- [ ] STORAGE BINS
- [ ] ALARM CLOCK
- [ ] PERSONAL FAN
- [ ] RUG
- [ ] PHONE

CLOTHING & ACCESSORIES
- [ ] SHIRTS/TOPS
- [ ] PANTS/SHORTS
- [ ] SWEATSHIRTS
- [ ] FORMAL ATTIRE
- [ ] WORKOUT CLOTHING
- [ ] UNDERWEAR
- [ ] SOCKS
- [ ] SHOES
- [ ] SLIPPERS
- [ ] BELT(S)
- [ ] PAJAMAS
- [ ] ROBE
- [ ] WATCH
- [ ] JEWELRY
- [ ] SHOWER SHOES
- [ ] WINTER GEAR
- [ ] SWIM GEAR
- [ ] RAIN GEAR

BATHROOM
- [ ] MOUTHWASH
- [ ] TOOTHBRUSH
- [ ] TOOTHPASTE
- [ ] DENTAL FLOSS
- [ ] RAZORS/SHAVING CREAM
- [ ] SHAMPOO/CONDITIONER
- [ ] SOAP/BODY WASH
- [ ] HAIR DRYER
- [ ] CHAPSTICK
- [ ] TWEEZERS
- [ ] COMB/BRUSH
- [ ] MAKEUP
- [ ] GLASSES /CONTACTS
- [ ] TAMPONS/PADS
- [ ] DEODORANT
- [ ] Q-TIPS
- [ ] NAIL CLIPPERS
- [ ] HAIR STYLING PRODUCTS
- [ ] PERFUME/COLOGNE
- [ ] SKIN MOISTURIZERS
- [ ] WASHCLOTHS & TOWELS
- [ ] PERSCRIPTION MEDICINE
- [ ] SHOWER CADDY

DESK & ACADEMIC
- [ ] STICKY NOTES
- [ ] DRY ERASE BOARD
- [ ] DESKTOP ORGANIZERS
- [ ] CALENDAR
- [ ] BACKPACK
- [ ] PENS AND PENCILS
- [ ] NOTEBOOKS/BINDERS
- [ ] LINED/BLANK PAPER
- [ ] PAPERCLIPS
- [ ] HOLE PUNCHER
- [ ] RULER
- [ ] FOLDERS
- [ ] STAPLER/STAPLES

HARDWARE & STORAGE
- [ ] HOOKS (ALL SIZES)
- [ ] SURGE PROTECTOR
- [ ] EXTENSION CORDS
- [ ] DUCT TAPE
- [ ] SHELVES & BRACKETS
- [ ] BOOKSHELVES
- [ ] CLOSET ORGANIZER
- [ ] SHELF & DRAWER LINERS
- [ ] CURTAINS & HARDWARE
- [ ] LIGHT BULBS
- [ ] TOOLS (HAMMER, SCREWDRIVER, NAILS)

ETHERNET CABLE
- [ ] TAPE
- [ ] ETHERNET CABLE
- [ ] COMPUTER
- [ ] EXTENSION CORD
- [ ] 2/3 PRONG ADAPTERS
- [ ] LAPTOP CASE/ BAG
- [ ] USB DRIVE
- [ ] PRINTER
- [ ] DESK LAMP
- [ ] CAMERA
- [ ] MP3 PLAYER

(top)
- [ ] SCISSORS
- [ ] INDEX CARDS
- [ ] STAMPS/ENVELOPES
- [ ] CALCULATOR

LAUNDRY/LINEN
- [ ] LAUNDRY DETERGENT
- [ ] BLEACH
- [ ] FABRIC SOFTENER
- [ ] LAUNDRY BAG/SORTER
- [ ] STAIN REMOVER
- [ ] IRON/IRONING BOARD
- [ ] STARCH
- [ ] HANGERS

CLEANING
- [ ] BROOM/MOP/VACUUM
- [ ] ALL-PURPOSE CLEANER
- [ ] CLEANING SPONGES
- [ ] FABRIC ODOR REMOVER
- [ ] AIR FRESHENER
- [ ] DISH LIQUID
- [ ] TRASH CAN
- [ ] TRASH BAGS

(top)
- [ ] DISH SOAP
- [ ] SCRUBBING PADS
- [ ] CAN OPENER
- [ ] PAPER TOWELS

SNACKING
- [ ] MINI-FRIDGE
- [ ] MICROWAVE

FIRST AID BOX
- [ ] BAND-AIDS
- [ ] ANTIBIOTIC OINTMENT
- [ ] TWEEZERS
- [ ] GAUZE / TAPE
- [ ] HYDROGEN PEROXIDE
- [ ] RUBBING ALCOHOL
- [ ] THERMOMETER
- [ ] ACE BANDAGE
- [ ] FREEZABLE ICE PACK

IMPORTANT DOCUMENTS
- [ ] DRIVER'S LICENSE
- [ ] SOCIAL SECURITY CARD
- [ ] BIRTH CERTIFICATE
- [ ] PASSPORT
- [ ] HEALTH INSURANCE INFORMATION

ACKNOWLEDGEMENTS

To Keyana Brown— I became a good person, student, and athlete because of the example and morals you showed me when I was a young boy. I finally got my 4.0 just like you even though it was thirteen years later. Thanks for everything you did for me growing up sis.

To Ms. Mary Elizabeth Jackson—without you, there would be no one to thank for my completion of this project. After spending less than an hour with me in the children's shelter, you took me home with you to Vallejo, California. Because you never gave up on me—no matter how many of your relatives told you to send me back because I was hopeless—I stand today as an example of what unconditional love and hope can do for a person.

I love you, and I thank you from the bottom of my heart. May you rest in peace.

Your Son,

-Kevin.

To my dearest Marie Elizabeth Dutton Brown—your guidance as a mother figure and mentor has been and continues to be a life-changing experience. You have believed in me since we met, and with your grace of the "412 Experience," this project is possible. I cannot describe the difference you have made in my life. To call you an angel is an understatement of what you are to the world and to me. I love you. Thank you for all that you do and most of all, thank you for being you, an *Original* in every sense of the word!

To Mr. Pelton Stewart—you started me off on the path to leadership with Torch Club (known as the Mighty Oaks Torch Club today) at the Continentals of Omega Boys and Girls Club. At the age of seven, you challenged me to keep at least one form of I.D., a watch (because I should always know what time it is), and to have knowledge of my local and federal government.

Torch club was a huge part of my foundation and you were the architect. Thank you for all of your hard work and dedication over the years.

To Mr. Philmore Graham—words cannot express the everlasting impact that you have on my life. At the age of nine, when I was constantly causing trouble and spending lots of time at the Continentals of Omega Boys and Girls Club, you saved my future. I remember the staff members wanting to give up on me but instead of allowing me to be kicked out of the club, you took the situation into your own hands and challenged me, starting with a question that I will never forget: "What weighs more? A pound of bricks or a pound of feathers?" After answering, "A pound of bricks," you explained to me that they both weighed a pound. From that day forward, you had my full attention. From that experience, you groomed me to understand the rewards and importance of education. The impact of "Study Hall," Keystone, Smart Moves training, the continental honor, and our walks on the Vallejo city waterfront all played a huge part in my making a conscious decision to stay on the road less traveled. I appreciate you for how you changed my life, Mr. Graham. Thank you!!!

To Ms. Carrie S. Wilson—you changed the course of my life after one of my high school basketball games when you asked, "Kevin Brown, are you going to college?" Through your tireless efforts and teachings, I achieved a higher education academically and continue to do so in life. Your teachings beyond the classroom have impacted me eternally, and I am forever grateful to have known Mr. Wilson (a terrific father figure), Kimberly, and Geoffrey. The Wilson family has shaped me. Thank you for everything; I love you all!!!

To Ms. Evelyn "Heart Lady" Polk—you are a mother figure and a positive role model in my life. Since meeting you at the Boys and Girls Club when I was in high school, you have encouraged me to maximize my potential. You started me on my way to New York in the summer of 2008 and are truly an angel with a huge heart. Thank you God Mom "E"!!!

To The Gross Family—Thank You for your continued support over the years, you inspired me to want more out of life.

To the Clark Atlanta University (CAU) staff and faculty you changed me from an eighteen-year-old kid fresh off of the plane from California to a well-traveled man of the world. Thank you for introducing me to our mantra "I'll Find A Way Or Make One." which helped me achieve a debt-free college education. Without you all, I truly would not be able to write this project. Thank you for helping me grow as a person. I would like to extend special thanks to Mrs. Dorothy Batey, Mr. Tolbert, Mr. Hickey, Mrs. Ragsdale, Ty from the print shop, Jason Richardson, Mrs. Morgan, Dr. Jenkins, Ms. Beverly Ferguson-Barrett, Dr. Muhammad Bhiuyan, Ms. Jackie Davis, Dr. Paul Brown, Dr. Dennis Kimbro and the rest of the staff that was present during my matriculation at CAU.

To Dr. Raphael Moffett — You are the best big brother a person can ever have. Every since the ice breaker we did my first week of college, to my request of you being my mentor, to waking up every morning at 7am to work out so I could make the basketball team and all of my other endeavors. You have been there every step of the way, for every accomplishment. Moff, your influences made my matriculation through Clark Atlanta a true growing experience and as I grow to know more about life you still impact me. Without you I would not be where I am today in the same style and fashion. Thank you for being a model for what a great man is and what a role model should be.

To Mrs. Dorothy Batey — An angel and mother figure. You stopped me from switching my major from Fashion Design and in return opened up the world of design to me. Your tireless work as a teacher and mentor in the fashion department is why I excelled as a CAU student in domestic and international study environments. Your standards and expertise have lit up the path and I can assure you that I will continue to follow it. Thank you so much for everything Mrs. Batey.

To Mr. Javier Tolbert —Thank you for your attention to detail and the high standard that you held all of your fashion design/merchandising students to. Because of your influence I understand professionalism, spacing and a standard that you would be proud of. I thank you for your influence and level of expectation. I promise to carry on this standard.

To all of my fellow CAU Panthers who continue to achieve—you push me to become better. Thank You!!!

To Mike Stu – Thank you for being a true friend over the years. From Vallejo to Atlanta, through my first clothing company KAY 1 Apparel and even in the present. You have always been a person that I can count on. I love you bro. I look forward to the future as we evolve.

To the Alvarez family—Thank you for introducing me to New York and for your continued family support throughout my journey.

To Lester Edwards—Thank you for your undying support and leadership through tremendous odds during my time working under you. You gave me the opportunity to remain in New York and follow my dreams. You are a great man.

To the Jackson family—Thank you for your continued love and support over the course of my life. The foundation was laid in my early years and you have been with me throughout my journey. - I love you all.

To John C. White—our initial conversation about this project encouraged me to see it through to completion. Thank you for always believing in me. Thank you for being my friend.

To Aleesha Nash (aka A. Nash) "The Legend"—my partner in grind, friend, and bawse, lol. Thank you for believing in this project and me. You have been on board since day one and your tireless efforts and sense of humor are greatly appreciated.

Twitter: @KevBrown1 | Facebook.com/KevBrown001

Thanks to your irreplaceable talents, this project was taken to unexpected heights and is possible. Thank you for being you and understanding "THE STANDARD" lol.

To Mario Shamir—Thank you for your creative genius.

To Shaun Derik, thank you for believing in me and this project, but most of all, thank you for your time spent encouraging me to live my dreams.

To my friend and brother Carl Bowen—thank you for your encouragement and support during this project.

To my friend and brother Eric Fondren—thank you for your encouragement and support during this project.

To Victoria Merriweather and Avia Hicks-Chapman—thank you both for your support on this project.

To Nick Ferris—thank you for allowing me to use your article "Ten Ways Anyone Can Go to College With Zero Student Loans" as a source of inspiration for this book. www.punnymoney.org is a great and humorous resource for financial management.

It is impossible to thank everyone who has influenced and offered me messages to share with others. So I apologize to all of my supporters, fans, and friends not listed here. I appreciate you.

To my current and future peers in the higher education realm— work hard to achieve the freedoms you deserve— especially the freedom of a debt-free college education.

To my current and future peers in the expert community—I am honored to be among you. This field is filled with individuals who inspire, and through teaching others, share their knowledge, experiences, and advice. To all: Continue to change lives.

ABOUT THE AUTHOR

Kevin Y. Brown is the founder of mydebtfreecollege.com and an authority on how to attend and graduate from college debt-free. He also lectures on personal identity and maximizing potential and resources.

By building and maintaining positive relationships with Clark Atlanta's professors and administrators, and doing all that was necessary to "meet everyone halfway," Kevin strategically made his way through college without student loan debt.

Since graduating, Kevin has been helping others identify resources for a debt-free college education.

Meet Kevin online and receive free college financial training at

www.mydebtfreecollege.com

Seminars by Kevin Y. Brown

AM/PM: As I Matriculate Pay Me!

Label Material Brand

Post College Freedom! (12 session program)

Start to Finish

StyleBook

Your Brand Within (10 session program)

Learn more about Kevin at

www.kevbrown1.com

BIBLIOGRAPHY

"About Us." *Student Aid on the Web*. Federal Student Aid, 30 June 2011. Web. 22 Oct. 2011. <http://studentaid.ed.gov/PORTALSWebApp/students/english/aboutus.jsp>.

"Consequences of Student Loan Default." *TG Online*. Texas Guaranteed Student Loan Corporation, 15 Sept. 2011. Web. 22 Oct. 2011. <http://www.tgslc.org/borrowers/default/consequences.cfm>.

"Federal Student Aid - Title IV Programs." *Federal Student Aid - Information on Grants, Student Loans, Scholarships and Other Financial Aid*. Federal Student Aid, 28 June 2010. Web. 22 Oct. 2011. <http://federalstudentaid.ed.gov/about/title4_programs.html>.

Julian, Tiffany A. and Robert A. Kominski. 2011. "Education and Synthetic Work- Life Earnings Estimates." *American Community Survey Reports*, ACS-14. U.S. Census Bureau, Washington, DC.

Kantrowitz, Mark Distribution of Debt at Graduation by Amount of Debt, College Type and Degree Program, September 29, 2010. (Addendum, October 1, 2010.

Kantrowitz, Mark. "FinAid | Loans | Defaulting on Student Loans." *FinAid! Financial Aid, College Scholarships and Student Loans*. Mark Kantrowitz. Web. 22 Oct. 2011. <http://www.finaid.org/loans/default.phtml>. (student loan default)

Kantrowitz, Mark. "FinAid | Student Loans." *FinAid! Financial Aid, College Scholarships and Student Loans*. Mark Kantrowitz. Web. 22 Oct. 2011. <http://www.finaid.org/loans/>.

"License Revocations | Student Loan Borrower Assistance." *Student Loan Borrower Assistance | A Resource for Borrowers, Their Families and Advocates*. National Consumer Law Center. Web. 22 Oct. 2011. <http://www.studentloanborrowerassistance.org/collections/government-collection-tools/license-revocations/>

U.S. Census Bureau 2012. "Table 293 INSTITUTIONS OF HIGHER EDUCATION-AVERAGE CHARGES" *12s0293.pdf*

INDEX